Developing the Afro-American Economy

Developing the Afro-American Economy

Building on Strength

Richard F. America

Lexington Books
D.C. Heath and Company
Lexington, Massachusetts
Toronto

Library of Congress Cataloging in Publication Data

America, Richard F
    Developing the Afro-American economy.

    Includes index.
    1. Afro-Americans—Economic conditions. 2. Afro-Americans—Social
conditions—1975— I. Title.
E185.8.A58   301.45'19'6073   76-54557
ISBN 0-669-01304-8

Published simultaneously in Canada

Printed in the United States of America

International Standard Book Number: 0-669-01304-8

Library of Congress Catalog Card Number: 76-54557

To my mother and father

Contents

List of Tables

Acknowledgments

The ideas in this book have developed over a decade, and they have been stimulated by many conversations, as well as by the observations of others. At Stanford Research Institute from 1965 to 1969 several colleagues, especially Bill Powers, Bob Arnold, Jerry Williams and Ben Lefkowitz, provided many hours of challenge and debate on a variety of public policy issues. At the University of California at Berkeley, Marcus Alexis, Chet McGuire, Ed Epstein and Ken Simmons were valuable sounding boards from time to time, as was Mike Winston at Howard University.

Other helpful colleagues include Professors Dow Votaw of Berkeley, Margaret Simms of Atlanta University, Bernard Anderson of The Wharton School, University of Pennsylvania, and Charles Anderson of Rutgers University, who read and critiqued parts of the manuscript. Professor Alfred Osborne of UCLA's Graduate School of Management—my coeditor on another and related project—also critiqued portions of this work.

Professor Jerald Udinsky of the Department of Economics at the University of California at Santa Cruz was of crucial assistance when, as a graduate student at Berkeley, he completed statistical estimations on income transfer through discrimination and looked into the potential in antitrust for redressing social overconcentration.

I benefited from the opportunity to present certain central ideas and to receive timely and insightful review at the Joint Center for Community Studies at UCLA in 1975 and at a seminar at the Center for the Study of Democratic Institutions in Santa Barbara in 1971. Also in 1971, the corporate transfer proposal was presented and reviewed by staff at a RAND Corporation seminar in Santa Monica, which was of substantial help in refining that concept.

Students in the economic development seminars at the Business School at University of California, Berkeley, and at Stanford Business School were always perceptive and critical, and for that I thank them.

Introduction

Over the next fifty years the focus of energy and attention in Afro America is going to be on development processes that will bring it into a condition of economic parity with the general American system.

Similar income and wealth distributions and a similar median income are objective targets. The organizations that have, up until now, been thought of primarily as civil rights, or social service, or activist organizations are going to evolve into developmental instruments. Their leadership will more and more adopt a managerial and developmental point of view, and will be drawn from backgrounds in policy analysis and management rather than the more traditional legal, religious, journalistic, social science and social service orientations of the past seventy-five years.

This book is a discussion of strategies and specific concerns that can be attended to by these organizations and by these leaders and managers. Much can be learned from traditional development processes that can be carefully applied in the developing Afro-American system with due regard for the obvious differences in circumstances and political setting.

An important element in this effort will be the determination, discipline, and esprit de corps of the population in the system. Also of importance, however, will be the degree of support from the general American system. Managing this relationship in a harmonious and effective manner will be a major task of the development leadership. One of the ongoing processes between the systems will be the redistribution of income and wealth based on the rationale of the social debt. This concept receives some attention in the middle portions of the book.

The following sections introduce specific proposals and techniques for managing the redistributive process with emphasis on the creation and sustenance of institutions and going concerns.

Finally, the development process will tend to bog down unless three special problems are successfully managed. The first is the problem of crime and misbehavior. Adequate standards of personal and collective conduct can be a major concern of leadership. Ways can be found to manage the problem of deterioration in behavior and for restoring high levels of respect for law and for justice in personal dealings by persons in all the population groups within the system.

The second problem is the management of the internal funding process for the many noncommercial activities that require continuing, financially reliable, and prudent support. The National Fund is the mechanism that can make possible many worthwhile projects and experimental efforts.

Finally, the management of the research and contract consulting process of public agencies at federal, state, and local levels is important. Careful attention can be paid to these activities, as they greatly affect public policy toward overall development efforts as well as the details of many minor components.

The adoption of the managerial and developmental point of view is timely as Afro America enters the last quarter of the twentieth century.

1

Managing General Development

Successful management of the development of Afro America requires that those institutions, communities, and individuals that are so frequently spoken of as "the black community" be viewed as a developing social, political, and economic system.

The Afro-American system includes all persons who the U.S. Census would enumerate as Negro or black, as well as a sizeable number missed by the Census. The system is comprehensive, encompassing suburban, urban, and rural activities and the rich as well as the middle class and the poor. It includes much more than the inner city "ghetto."

It may be worthwhile to anticipate immediately a reaction of some economists to a proposed public policy of encouraging development. They would ask whether the kind of development proposed is socially efficient.

There are two principal bases from which to argue for such development. The first is on grounds of economic efficiency, and the second derives from considerations of equity, fairness, and social stability. The policy prescription for development relies heavily, but not exclusively, on equity rationales for support.

Efficiency rationales assume that the general American system, i.e., the nation as a whole, would benefit from this development—which up to now has been viewed by most policy analysts and economists as primarily a process of job creation—because it would be efficient. Government expenditures on many job-creating aspects of business and community development could, of course, be justified on economic grounds. Large successful business and cooperative enterprises in inner city communities could help reduce unemployment, reduce welfare dependency, boost and refresh deteriorating areas, diminish criminal activity, and increase economic and social stability. But unlike some other analyses, the managerial view here views job creation as only a very important part of the development process, not the end in itself.

1

A reliance on efficiency rationales and on overriding concern for employment also tends to be associated with a high sensitivity to possible adverse political reactions to development proposals. Sensitivity to political reality is wise, and an attempt to manage proposals in such a way that they can appeal to a wide range of potential political support is prudent. But in the development process there will inevitably be resistance because success will mean reallocation of public and private resources. It is worthwhile attempting to manage the process in a politically realistic manner, but the development leadership cannot hope to avoid all conflict with established interest groups.

A case for many aspects of development can be made on grounds of allocative efficiency. But there seem to be some business leaders, professional economists, journalists, and political leaders who are open only to such arguments. They will probably tend to resist those aspects of what is proposed that can be clearly labeled redistributive.

The second basis on which to rest development proposals—equity and social stability—is also strong, and it has important historical precedents.

Comprehensive public policies to revitalize cities and reduce general poverty and related social dysfunction rest on both equity and efficiency bases. It is a matter of equity when government policy seeks to correct housing, employment, health, and capital ownership deficiencies, and in most cases ways can be found to do these things efficiently. Furthermore, doing them successfully is presumed to have as one payoff increased general social efficiency.

Suffice to say that natural development has been hindered over several generations by socially and economically motivated opposition. Credit has been restricted, and government policy has been indifferent or hostile. Education and especially on-the-job training in high skill and managerial categories has been for the most part unavailable. So equity now calls for accelerated opportunities to acquire capital and training. These can be provided most effectively if private and public sector policy makers view the entire process as one of system development rather than merely the running of isolated and unrelated programs.

Economic development in the domestic situation is a process that can be heavily concerned with the attainment of important non-economic, social, and political objectives. Political strength, as has often been observed, can extract economic concessions from an adversary. This new economic clout in turn can then be used to produce additional political leverage, leading to still further economic benefit. In the view of some observers, this boils down to basic politics and to a set of political economic notions about bargaining behavior and about how public resources are actually allocated through the political process in a society like the United States. Those observers and analysts who put heavy emphasis on efficiency considerations are tending to overlook these political aspects of the process. In managing development, it can be prudent to put appropriate emphasis on just such aspects.

The managerial point of view rests on the premise that for the majority of all Americans, the development of this system is desirable, and it is probably substantially technically achievable by the year 2020.

2

Building the System: Analogies to Traditional Development

In the middle 1960s interest in business development began to rise. During the decade following, federal programs and private corporate and foundation experiments helped stimulate that interest, and significant business benefits have been derived from these efforts.

During the presidential election campaign in 1968, Richard Nixon suggested that his administration would pay attention to supporting the development of "minority business enterprise." And the administration did follow through to some extent. Federal attention was focused on aiding entrepreneurial activities. An important rationale was that this would generate jobs. Business development was viewed by politicians, federal officers, business leaders, and many journalists and academicians as desirable, primarily because of its expected value as an employment technique. But by 1970 it was becoming apparent that, relative to the need for jobs, little employment generation could realistically be expected from this source in the near term. The workforce impact was generally agreed to have been disappointing.

Not only was the focus during 1969–1970 on small business and the hope for more jobs to be thereby created, but the primary geographic locus for business creation was in the inner city. As it turned out, programs and policies based on these three concepts—inner city location, small-scale business, and job creating—proved to be inadequate responses to the widely expressed desire for the creation of competitive businesses.

These programs lacked adequate funding, some of their sponsors in the Administration and in Congress were ambivalent about how much success they really wished to see in these activities, and some of the administrators in the agencies, including SBA and others, were privately hostile to business development programs on a large and significant scale that would truly accelerate the progress of the developing systems. They were willing to provide modest support to small efforts often located in the inner city, and rationalized on the

5

basis of employment potential, but were not enthusiastic about programs that would transfer resources from the general to the developing systems on a large scale or that would produce serious cometition for firms in the general system. A good deal of cynicism pervaded the administration of many of these programs. Lastly Afro America's leadership had not carefully thought through the significance of business development to overall development, and some important established figures were opposed to committing sizeable resources to these efforts seeing in them conservative Republican political biases favoring small business over employment and training and especially public sector employment.

Lastly there really was a short supply of adequately trained and experienced managers and entrepreneurs ready to establish or take over and run successful and fully competitive businesses. "We can't find many who are qualified" has been a song of the opposition in many spheres for many years. But in business development for many reasons there really has been a short supply. This condition is being corrected, but it was a contributing factor to the lack of acceleration and partial failure of the business development programs of the 1968-1976 period.

There has been ample discussion of other factors that limited the potential in those programs; their general operating environment, weaknesses in their markets, problems with their products, capitalization, strategies, planning, structures, and so on. Further amplification would be redundant. Suffice to say that small business creation of that kind is only a worthwhile component of a much more ambitious comprehensive development program, not a development strategy in itself.

As a consequence, the notion of economic development in something approaching its classic form, while allowing for obvious differences in setting, and in legal and political realities, has emerged to capture the attention of many serious participants.

An Alternative Conception

During the early 1970s a substantial number of business people, government officials, analysts, and legislators were coming to agree that development should be something considerably more comprehensive than simply a process of inner city small-business creation. The concept that has been emerging calls for the development of a system of small, medium, and large businesses and cooperatives located wherever it makes economic and political sense. This includes, of course, agricultural and industrial development in the rural North and South. The concern is for the establishment of a vigorous economic community—a nationwide system of institutions developed, so far as is practicable, according to at least a suggestive set of plans. This concept recognizes the very high degree of interdependence such a system would have with the general American economy. There is also an element of self-conscious self-interest about such an idea that may provoke opposition. It can, however, readily accommodate itself to political and social realities through the rest of the twentieth century.

The Range of Development Preferences

A number of thoughtful observers in Afro America might find it difficult to embrace this development concept, feeling that it is too moderate. The spectrum of opinion there on economics, as in politics and social and cultural affairs, can be arranged into roughly five groupings: separatist, radical reformist, moderate reformist, assimilationist, and, fifth, a number of groups who express a desire or intention to see some sort of large-scale change in American society through what is commonly, and often imprecisely, called "revolution." Such an easy sketchy outline is, of course, open to probing question, and it is obviously vulnerable to fair-minded criticism from all sides. It is useful here only to provide a way to identify what may be judged to be the majority of those actively working in development. They seem to be interested in moderate reforms, with a few important exceptions who are working for what would generally be seen as a more radical program. Those business people, on the other hand, whose only apparent concern is entrepreneurial activity, can be fairly placed between moderate reform and assimilation. And, generally speaking, those who oppose any approach that relies at all on "free enterprise capitalism," even if substantially mixed with community-based efforts, can probably be classified, and would most often identify themselves, as radical or "revolutionary" in some sense.

Those working in economic development range along the philosophical spectrum but seem to be concentrated in the moderate middle not unexpectedly. It is a good guess, however, that they are generally politically more progressive than business people in general at least on those issues that have been associated with liberal politics of the last two generations. This may, of course, simply mean that the liberal position on those issues happens to coincide with their perceived self-interest and that at bottom most are about as personally conservative as most small business operators, business-oriented civil servants, journalists, academics, and other business support professionals.

So the program outlined here seeks substantial but moderate reform. It is, after all, concerned with orderly management. It does, however, anticipate far-reaching tax and budget changes that will encourage development. And it assumes that, though there will be continuing social conflict, there will also be a reasonably high level of cooperation with the general American system.

The Race Issue and Public Policy

For many years, and most intensely during the decade of the 1960s, there was argument, protest, and petition for redress of a number of grievances. Those actions contributed to producing important benefits in legal safeguards and material advancement. Nevertheless, there remain obstacles to national harmony. And it is reasonable to suppose that conflict will continue to result because of the residue of untreated problems and the apparent and rather natural determination of some well-placed groups and individuals to try to maintain disproportionate economic and political advantages.

There are two principal aspects of this social dynamic that seem to contribute to continuing difficulties. The first is mutual mistrust. This has declined somewhat, but it remains serious despite rising incomes, free access to public accommodations, and a more even-handed administration of justice. All these advances increase the probabilities of harmonious living. But while they are necessary, they are apparently not sufficient conditions for stable trust.

The second, and related aspect, is a widespread feeling of insecurity in Afro America. There seems to be a general view that predatory dominant economic behavior, and a continuing inclination toward abuse of authority cannot be held in check solely by recourse to the courts and the governmental apparatus. Security is an issue, and it is a phenomenon that can be usefully viewed as not un-like the concern for national security of sovereign states. Security in this situation, it is felt, will depend on developing strength of various kinds—individual, religious, familial, legal, political, cultural, and economic. Some large institutions in the general system such as labor unions, trade associations, corporations, political organizations, even professional and educational associations, whose activities are some-times harmful, must be constrained, according to this view, by a credible possibility of retaliation. This kind of exercise of economic and political strength is the sort of thing that has been recognized in various theories of countervailing power.

Is it, however, in the general public interest; would it be sound and prudent public policy to use public resources to foster such countervailing power? There seems to be a growing conviction among analysts that the answer to this perplexing question is yes. Social conflict cannot be eliminated soon, but it can be managed; it can be channeled into confined expression. Let it occur in the courts, in markets, and in political life. It is, therefore, in the public interest to make sure that all parties have the institutional tools to engage in fair conflict. The logic goes on that in addition to legal, political, and social institutions, economic ones are also important in this context.

Economic institutions, such as privately owned businesses, in addition to doing business, also act politically, at least locally, even if only indirectly. They influence political outcomes on land use, edu-cation, taxation, and other important local issues on behalf of some-body. And this will continue to be so with such institutions that develop in the Afro American system. These business units, it is be-lieved, will help reduce their communities' overdependence on the general system and its institutions, many of which are still widely perceived as untrustworthy.

Distributing the Gains from Development

Normally, in the lagging and unindustrialized sectors of the world, development has been preoccupied with providing infrastruc-ture—utilities, housing, transportation, education, health—and producing per capita income gains. Because of the unique features of this development process, the first would be of less concern than in traditional circumstances, and the second would be an objective to be achieved largely indirectly through the general workings of the economy.

Infrastructure, or social overhead capital, is already widely available throughout the United States, for the most part. Maintenance and innovation of utilities, transportation, health, educational systems, and so on can remain a priority concern, but there is not an absolute lack of any of these. The development process will not be hampered by the traditional problem of woefully inadequate infrastructure.

Most of the labor force will continue to remain on payrolls of the general system, public and private. Income gains will therefore be tied to the economic soundness of the general system. Development of business in Afro America will probably not provide a great increase in direct employment for lower-income people in the next ten years, although, of course, some jobs will be created by this process for these groups. But there is a desire to bring about rapid income and employment gains for the lowest-income groups. How can that be done? Sources of income and employment increase will be these: full employment in the general system and increased income redistribution through transfer payments, social security, various allowances to those in real need, health programs, housing subsidies, and the like.

An important function of the business institutions that develop, then, will be to participate in the local, state, and national political process and press for that redistribution. Largely through this indirect but potentially highly productive manner, development, and especially in this case, business development, will bring about income gains for the most economically deprived.

Further sustained analysis may reveal greater opportunities for practicable labor-intensive business development with resulting direct income gains. At the moment, however, such opportunities are not apparent. The course described will probably turn out to be the most effective through the next decade.

Requisites for Development

There are several important components that seem to have been present in most effective general development programs. It will be helpful to look at six that have not received the explicit attention in public debate that they deserve in consideration of development processes. Development managers can make more frequent reference to such factors in future deliberations.

Nationalism

In some constructive form, the element generally called nationalism seems to have been present wherever successful development has been accomplished. Perhaps this is just an appearance and not a true development prerequisite. There is a possibility of *post hoc ergo propter hoc* reasoning. Nevertheless, it is safe to assert carefully that some effective degree of widely felt nationalistic feeling will be necessary if development is to be realized. Let us be clear; by nationalism is meant a constructive sense of group purpose, not any virulent or fanatical display of hostility toward others.

Some of the media, in the past, have been inclined or drawn to focus on various dramatic, and usually youthful, manifestations of aggressive behavior. This has been headlined as "nationalism." What we are considering here is instead a mature emotion. In the context of a developing system within an advanced developed society such as the United States, it might simply be called pride or community spirit. But to be of importance and functional with respect to development, it must be extensive and of sufficient intensity to motivate extra effort and financial sacrifice by many people on behalf of some reasonable set of collective objectives. Something like a voluntary tax program, or National Fund, and increased donations to sound, well-managed, community-based development efforts by the middle and upper classes will be necessary to development. Unless such a practical form of nationalism exists or can be generated, it is probably not worthwhile thinking seriously of comprehensive economic and community development.

Savings

Next, and related, is the requirement for capital accumulation and savings generation. That this is an essential development ingredient has been widely recognized for some time. Charismatic and religious leaders have historically succeeded in inducing some consumption restraint and relatively large contributions by their lower-income followers. The question now is, can the aspiring middle class—encouraged to conspicuous consumption—make the conscious decision to delay some gratification and increase savings, even as its income rises? The savings rate will have to increase if development is to occur and be sustained.

If meaningful development investment strategies are to succeed at supporting strong businesses and corporations, there will also have to be some shifts of deposits from financial institutions in the general system to banks in the Afro American system. For a decade or so that will mean acceptance by some depositors of greater inconvenience and at least some short-run increase in risk. Development depends on the willingness of enough people to make such reasonable changes in economic behavior.

Planning

Planning still seems to be a dirty word for many leaders in the general American business world who tend to associate it with socialism and with centralized governmental investment and operating decisions. Some professional planning function will have to be established in several private or semipublic agencies if there is really a serious interest in efficient allocation of financial resources and rapid development. But since there is no legal or political mechanism that can enforce planning decisions, what will be meaningful about plans developed by, say, the NAACP, or the National Urban League, or the National Business League that rely wholly on voluntary acceptance? A satisfactory answer to this fundamental question is simply not yet available. Clearly much more analytical attention can be devoted to the need for planning and to organizational approaches to planning. It may be that lagging urban centers such as Harlem, the South Side, and Watts cannot really develop into stable and broadly attractive communities unless the rural South develops simultaneously or in some carefully determined sequence according to a rational integrated plan and program. Some such comprehensive planning process is going to be necessary to prevent investment and management attention from being focused myopically on only local and parochial development issues.

A Management Cadre

The emergence of a commercial leadership group—a broad management cadre—must occur early in the development process. This class must be well-educated, broadly experienced, dedicated to individual and group development, and well compensated. Its members can supply energy, vision, and commitment not only to their own enterprises, but also to the overall development effort. Because opportunities for advanced education and on-the-job training in management have only recently become available in any quantity, it is likely that a continuing and severe shortage of management talent will be experienced until the early 1980s.

One of the recurring criticisms of the "black capitalism" thrust of the early 1970s was that "a few individuals would get rich." This was thought to be undesirable and was to be avoided: "We don't want to develop a group of millionaires who merely exploit their own people." This theme, largely based on a straw man—internal exploitation—seems to die hard. Exploitation through the generation of excess profits, made possible by monopoly pricing or depressed wages, is an evil that can be combatted throughout the society. But the concept of generous rewards for jobs well done by managers and entrepreneurs should not be placed under an ideological cloud. If strong institutions and a viable system are to be developed, there will unavoidably have to be generous financial incentives to the skilled, highly trained, management leadership group that will be indispensable in that effort. They need not flaunt their earnings. Hopefully, they will, for the most part, have that sense of collective purpose spoken of earlier that will give them some social discipline and will permit them to forego voluntarily some of the material privileges and perquisites that mark the lifestyle of the commercial elite in the general society. There is a clear and striking need for a management and technical leadership class, but not for a financial and industrial elite or an oligarchy in the traditional sense. If these social and behavioral distinctions can be kept clear, the development task can be made simpler, because status conflicts that can be crippling and even immobilizing will be minimized.

Development is a matter of building on strength. Correcting weaknesses is an important objective and must also be a continuing concern effectively managed. But acceleration of the development process requires that the strongest cultural traits be identified and the strongest assets and individuals harnessed. Those with advanced education and training, of quality, in the necessary management and technical fields are going to be of great value. And many of them are going to be individually enriched beyond their early expectations. It seems that many lenders, consultants, foundation officials and board members, academics, journalists, and high civil servants and elected officials both in Afro America and in the general society are deeply troubled by or firmly opposed to development policies and programs that will have as one consequence the further enrichment of middle class people who are already well off. It is believed, apparently, that some way can be found to achieve the development of the bulk of the people in Afro America while preventing any direct immediate benefits to the managers, leaders and entrepreneurs. It is also believed, for example, that there is no justification for an SBA or foundation or private banking policy that gives extra assistance to a high-income, black loan applicant. Aside from the rationale of the Social Debt to be discussed later and elaborated separately, development cannot be achieved without the rewarding involvement of the technically and managerially talented. They will create and lead institutions that will benefit others and society as a whole, and in so doing they will benefit personally. That is not an undesirable or unjustifiable social-policy outcome.

In any event, building on strength is the key to development. Many of those who resist any proposals if they appear to potentially enrich the already strong, are of course, privately dubious about or hostile to the whole idea of systemic development. They will support individual opportunity, but see no persuasive social-policy rationale for developing the Afro-American system, as such. They are beyond the reach of this argument, and in fact are opposed. This is addressed to those who want to see development and agree with the general objective of economic parity, but who are troubled by the prospect of enrichment of the strong as a by product of that process.

It can also be clear that any skilled managers, regardless of race, who understand and accept the premises underlying this development effort, and who can function effectively with the Afro-American leaders of this effort, can make a contribution. Xenophobia, paranoia, and bigotry are harmful to any development effort and have no place in this one. Good faith offers of management and technical talent can be accommodated both as a matter of principle and as a practical matter.

Entrepreneurship

If development is going to accelerate enough to take off, it will require the active presence of a group of risk takers and venturers, in addition to skilled managers and high-level technicians. Entrepreneurial spirit perhaps can be taught in the classroom or on the job, and it may in some cases be contagious. It is impossible to know the available supply of entrepreneurial types or whether it is adequate to sustain a flow of new, successful businesses. But despite the lack of a strong existing commercial base, there is evidence that a substantial venture spirit exists. It may only need a slightly more congenial climate in order to flourish. If that is so, then the problem becomes largely political—to see to the availability of the necessary public and private inducements and supports.

Creativity

The last of these six development prerequisites is technical creativity—the presentation of new products and services through organized professional research and development. The next four to five decades in the United States will see a great expansion of the knowledge industry, including universities and other training centers, endowed and contract research centers, and corporate research. New products and services that will provide the basis for much economic growth will be conceived and perfected there. Afro America can also look to its higher educational system—its principal research-oriented universities—and to its individuals engaged throughout the general system and can create an independent research capability to organize information and generate knowledge on behalf of economic progress.

Indeed, some confusion has been generated around the debate over what to do about the 120-odd junior and four year colleges and universities in the higher educational system in Afro America. What is their function, how shall they be supported, which shall be permitted to perish and which shall be strengthened and relied on. Apparently, these issues have been approached as if they were simply educational questions. They are not. They are economic issues as well. Those schools are not only educational institutions, they are also economically productive units. They educate and train individuals, but they can also be useful in producing human capital and knowledge, to the extent that some are research oriented. The United Negro College Fund (UNCF), for example, conducts a fund-raising campaign, designed largely by the Advertising Council, as a public service, that makes an appeal based on the merits of individual student need. Perhaps this is effective and philosophically comfortable. An alternative, however, would be an appeal that recognized at least certain schools as being economic units and elements in a network of economic institutions including banks and businesses, fund-raising mechanisms, and planning and research units. "A Mind Is A Terrible Thing To Waste" may be effective, as an appeal to compassion. But the UNCF might find it worthwhile to conduct a campaign that projects the institutions as economically productive units in a development process, and that are necessary components of a comprehensive system. Similarly, those foundation executives and educational administrators who are concerned about efficient management of this subsystem of colleges and universities can sharpen their analysis by considering how the institutions figure in a systemic development program.

The advanced industrial countries are moving out of and beyond the industrial age into a period that is often called postindustrial. This period will be characterized by important changes in some of the deepest personal values of large masses of people. There will also be changes in the way goods and services are produced and marketed. Furthermore, over the next fifty years, some of the currently important rules of general economic life—including working customs, the use of currency, and so on—will have changed substantially. Important aspects of the industrial organization of that time may be barely recognizable from the perspective of the 1970s. So in undertaking development, leaders and managers can keep these virtually certain changes in mind so as to avoid the unexpectedly rapid obsolescence of newly created enterprises.

To summarize, the management of development will require a recognition of the importance of six development requirements:

nationalism, savings, planning, management, entrepreneurship. and creativity. Two other guidelines can also be of value.

Development Guidelines

In the period 1967–1970 a great deal of discussion was devoted to the question of how to make areas like Harlem, Bedford-Stuyvesant, Roxbury, and so on more self-contained economically. During the early 1970s the realization of the low probability of success of that attempt in the near future apparently dissuaded most advocates.

Interest has now been focused on how to develop successful companies wherever physically located—in city, or suburb, or beyond—and how to create and sustain economic security. Two general guidelines can be useful in reviewing legislation, administrative regulations, and specific development programs at state and local levels. It is useful to determine whether the eventual thrust of a program or proposal will be primarily to encourage "import" substitution or "export" creation.

"Import Substitution"—Buying Internally Produced Goods and Services

Much of the popular and professional interest in a "self-contained" economy grew out of a desire to restrain somehow the consumption of "imported" goods and services. That is, a natural and universal impulse in development efforts that within limits can be constructive. Some shifts in consumption to "home" sources can probably be induced on the basis of an appeal to spirit—"buy Afro-American"— even if not on the basis of more attractive price and quality. Capturing some of those expenditures and diverting them to internal development is usually an important part of a comprehensive strategy. The two economies we are concerned with, however, the general system and the Afro-American system, are, in fact, highly interdependent and, for many if not most practical purposes, will be indistinguishable.

For the majority of people in Afro America, import substitution can probably best be accomplished in the consumption of food, clothing, shelter, and certain local services. Consumer durables, most luxuries, and most producers' goods, as a practical matter, must continue to be "imported." But even so, a steadily increasing share of the supplying of some of those essentials over the next four or five decades will produce a healthier trade balance.

Export Creation—Finding New Things to Sell to the
General American Public and to the Rest
of the World

There are some additional important business opportunities in the creation of certain kinds of "exports." The development of new products and services and the fresh organizing, packaging, and pricing of some older traditional services, including a number of low-skilled personal, domestic, and household services for export, can provide an economic stimulus.

An economic boost can also be derived from the increasing practice of importing intermediate or semifinished products, performing new work on them, and exporting the finished goods. In this process, high added value is the factor that leads to the increase in export volume. The development strategy with export creation, then, is not import substitution as such, but rather a change in the mix of products bought or "imported" by businesses to reflect a higher proportion of raw materials and semifinished goods. The finished products flowing to the general public from this activity form the basis for the export sector of the system.

Conclusion

A rationale for a program of broad system development has now been outlined, and we see that it can be readily considered to be in the general public interest and in the interest of Afro America. The process calls for substantial and sustained government financial support and also, very importantly, broad-based internal sacrifice, discipline, and extra effort.

It is becoming clear that serious and comprehensive development deserves wide and bipartisan support over the next four to five decades. The large majority of Americans can realize long-term benefits from such a policy.

3

Development in the Context of American Realities

As noted, despite substantial progress, there remains some social conflict and mistrust in the United States, and it may continue in various forms and with fluctuating intensity for another generation or so. Specialists on conflict have studied and given sustained formal attention to problems of international conflict, as well as to conflict domestically. Some note parallels between international conflict and bargaining, on the one hand, and domestic social conflict on the other. It would be preferable to treat domestic conflict simply with broad good will and creative cooperation. But scarce resources are at stake, and there are vested interests in the general system that will be diminished as Afro America approaches parity. So continued resistance can be expected. The practical problem is to make sure that conflict leads in the end to good faith bargaining, which in turn can produce reasonable economic concessions, appropriate political rearrangements, and carefully determined income and wealth redistribution.

The federal government has previously taken an active and conscious role in allowing, and even in supporting, the consolidation of the kind of countervailing social and economic strength that development will produce. Consider, for example, the development and consolidation of trade union strength in the 1930s. In that period a public policy evolved that held that support of union power, to protect labor from management abuse, and to produce material benefits for large numbers of workers, was a preferable course to either governmental nonsupport or opposition to the growing strength of the labor movement. This latter course, it was felt, was inequitable and also would have risked great social and political conflict, or at least a period of undesirable unrest.

So social system conflict and the development and acquisition of institutionalized strength are important background issues in considering strategies of economic development. A desire to correct for historic economic exploitation and the maldistribution of income and wealth are other underlying concerns that produce a determination to develop.

By now there is hardly an interested person who has not seen sufficient statistical summary of relative economic positions to be persuaded that there remains a substantial disparity. The ratio of black to white median income in 1975 was about 60 percent. The causes of the disparity, however, seem to remain a mystery to many. Managers and administrators tend to be practical people, relatively uninterested in abstractions like the historical causes of contemporary inequality. They may function in their jobs with greater vision, however, if they retain some interest in how these discrepancies came to be. And by being mindful of the big picture, they can be more inclined to add their efforts to broad social corrective processes.

Even in the event of substantial redistribution of income and wealth, however, and a narrowing of income differentials, institutional development will continue to be a necessary process because of the problems related to feelings of security and mistrust. Such positive economic steps toward social renewal might help remove some of the basis for distrust and insecurity problems. But it seems unlikely that broad progressive social policy will be adopted simply on the basis of persuasion and a general perception of enlightened self-interest. More likely, as the nineteenth century development leader, Frederick Douglass, observed, it will continue to be necessary that the general system's normal inertia first be reduced through the process of political conflict—"Agitation"—and bargaining, through both broad public debate and the electoral process.

4 The Development Perspective

The managers of development organizations can benefit from paying attention to some of the technical detail of programs in the development worlds of Asia, Africa, and Latin America. In the context of Afro-American development, the analogs, many of which were presented earlier, should be apparent.

For example, educational issues may be clarified if they are viewed as development issues. How can education be made achievement-oriented? The puzzling problems of urban public education in the United States raise the same sort of questions as are faced in some developing nations. What can be done to identify, systematically, early or later, those persons with a high need to achieve, and how can their ability be harnessed to produce economic benefits? Public education may have been systematically thwarting the economically important need to achieve in many children. Educators, journalists, and others can learn to assess educational issues in light of development requirements. Debate over educational policy in the cities has largely missed this fundamental issue, and this may be a large part of the reason for widespread unease about the processes of mass education.

Education

In considering the detailed requirements in development, the work of Sir Arthur Lewis may be instructive. His studies of capital accumulation in the traditional context prompt the question here of how much of total income goes into education? There are no formal estimates uncovered in this research, but if the total is less than 3 percent, that is less than $1 billion out of over $60 billion, how can it be raised? And, in any event, would a sustained level of 3 percent be sufficient to help accomplish a development objective of economic parity by the year 2020? Of course, the American educational system is financially integrated, and to a great extent common revenue pools are available to all, although this has been the subject of contention and court action. Taxes from Afro America help finance education in the general system and vice versa. So the parallel to an independent system, such as in a sovereign nation, is not very close or precise. But by looking at education as a development issue, the basic question can be raised: what are appropriate levels of investment in human capital and how can these levels be achieved?

Law and Order

And what is to be made of Lewis' statement that law and order is a foundation of economic growth? A lengthy look at crime and development will follow in a later section. There has been some perversion of that phrase—law and order—in popular discussion in the United States, and some cynicism has grown up around it. But it is probably the case that development cannot be achieved unless all citizens are able to maintain an adequate level of self-control and discipline. Common criminality, hoodlumism, juvenile delinquency, and degenerate behavior of all kinds very likely must be reduced to some minimum tolerable level in order for development to occur.

Planning

As a practical matter, as earlier asserted, planning is essential to satisfactory comprehensive development. It is worthwhile, however, to maintain a distinction between the creation of a formal development plan and the process of development planning. The latter is what the development managers can seek to establish, but planning is usually a government function. What, then, is to substitute for a government? Perhaps civil rights organizations, or a national organization of business people, or a broadly based chamber of commerce or business league. A third option would be a national organization of elected officials—local, state, and federal. The best approach may turn out to be a new conception of the NAA and NUL as development organizations with planning responsibilities, rather than as civil rights organizations. However it is set up, the operating question for the managers and development leaders will be how incentives can be devised and provided to encourage broad popular conformity to plans.

Perhaps instead of the production of plans as such, there is needed only a series of well-conceived development projects that can attract public and private resources. The important thing may be to organize effectively for a realistic level of coordinated critical investment in key businesses through both acquisitions and startups, bearing in mind the constraints placed by antitrust law on any collaborations in economic activity.

Qualifications

All this raises the problem of professional managerial qualifications in the development leadership. As amply demonstrated in the last ten years, unqualified persons appointed for political reasons to important jobs in development organizations cause waste of resources, missed opportunities, deteriorating morale, and failure. Cronyism is an enemy of development.

The problem of producing an effective managerial class is being faced, and accomplishing the transfer of know-how from the general system to the technicians and managers in the developing system appears to be succeeding.

Entrepreneurs

Where are the potential entrepreneurs? The source for the bulk of future entrepreneurs may be the offspring of the stable working class, rather than in the more professionally or managerially oriented middle class. In the meantime, a generation of businesses has apparently been spawned that has come to rely on a variety of federal, state, and local support programs. Set asides, technical assistance, favorable financing, and other aids to infant industries have been used to help firms get on their feet. It may now have become the case, however, that many, if not most, of these businesses will find it psychologically, as well as commercially difficult, if not impossible, to venture out without such support mechanisms. Successfully moving into the general competitive business environment may not be realized by very many firms until a second or third generation of entrepreneurs has been trained who have only faint memories of the government programs of the late 1960s and early to mid-1970s. A different sense of themselves as competitive business people, rather than primarily as pioneers and experimenters in an alien and hostile environment may be necessary for real business success. And because of the fact that they will not see themselves quite so uniquely as pioneers, they may find it easier to cooperate with and trust each other. Real mutual assistance and reduced suspicions will be beneficial to the individuals and to the collective effort.

In the first generation, for complex reasons, valuable opportunities to progress through sharing and cooperation were missed. The reasons for distrust and noncooperation include, jealousies, and envy, feelings of personal insecurity based on perceived lack of competence, philosophical and ideological differences, local political rivalries, long standing organizational disputes over turf, and issues of social psychology too involved to examine here. Exaggerated feelings of competitiveness, some hyper individualism, and a kind of entrepreneurial machismo also probably contributed. Indeed, some unconscious dynamics and rivalries involving unresolved intrapsychic conflict with no particular racial or social dimension may also have been factors in some instances. Some of the intrigue and apparent treachery that stood in the way of cooperation may also have had to do with the fact this was all occuring during an administration that subsequently was exposed as having a greater than normal taste for machievellian procedures. Some of this undoubtedly rubbed off on the programs of small business and minority enterprise and on some of the managers of those programs in the headquarters offices and in the field and regional offices. Finally, some of the difficulty arose because of the classic problem of scrapping over crumbs. These programs were not budgeted at serious levels or organized and supported in a way designed to make them truly successful. Participants were therefore put in the position of scrambling for inadequate resources, and this alone can cause unpleasantness, and did.

This need not be a permanent condition. The crabs in the barrel phenomenon may not be widespread, but it is common enough to cause many to experience difficulties that they might have avoided with a little more help from knowledgeable friends. The trade associations, business leagues, and the cooperation and technical assistance available through some of the Minority Enterprise Small Business Investment Companies (MESBICs), and other financing vehicles have been of increasing value to many. There seems to be, despite this, a high residue of mutual suspicion, and this is a hindrance. Perhaps it will only be reduced by time, experience, the example of greater success through cooperation, and the emergence of the next generation of more relaxed and personally more secure entrepreneurs.

Resource Reallocation

Some developing countries have sought to accelerate the process by expropriating facilities and other investments made in them by foreign investors. Indeed, this appears to be a widespread impulse. It also seems to exist in the United States. It can be plausibly argued that the rebellions in major cities during 1965–1968 were motivated in part by a desire to see the investments of nonlocal people taken over.

The development phenomenon of attempted capital takeover is nearly universal. There is usually some feeling among those seeking to develop that the foreign ownership rights on local property are questionable and can be traced to illegitimate and coercive transactions in the not too distant past. So expropriation is a favorite acquisition technique in many developing circumstances.

There is a serious and related question whether development can succeed in Afro America without some important asset transfers. They will, of course, have to be legal, fully compensated, and widely agreed to. The transfer of going concerns can perhaps be accomplished using the corporate transfer technique to be described subsequently.

Discouraging Imports

Programs of "aid" to Afro America are often designed to increase imports by it. Business managers in the general system are often concerned and supportive of domestic social reforms because of a belief that raising the incomes of lower-income groups will be reflected later in increased sales of goods and services to those groups. But as we have seen, the management of successful development may require instead that such imports be discouraged and minimized and, instead, that savings be encouraged and increased.

Agribusiness

A movement for development and for a measure of autonomy and security is usually related to a strong, and perhaps fundamentally instinctive, desire for some territorial control. Economic and political control in the so-called Southern "black belt" has been an objective in many minds for many years. Now, in the context of overall development, there is evidence of renewed interest in agriculture in this region and in participation in agribusiness nationwide. The population of the states on the Gulf and the South Atlantic is 30 to 40 percent black, with majorities in many counties. Eleven and one-half million black people live in the South, almost 50 percent of the national total, and about five million of those live in rural areas.

As a policy matter, agricultural development here is, in many ways, a problem of land reform. Much of the land resided on in the belt from Virginia to Texas is absentee-owned or, if owned by the residents, has not been efficiently managed. Development managers can concentrate on acquiring title to desired land. American agriculture is technically and organizationally advanced, but there are similarities in land tenure patterns to those in some developing countries, and land reform is a priority matter in Afro America as it is elsewhere.

There are related policy issues having to do with population and migration policy that can also draw the attention of the development managers. The questions of who shall leave the land and where shall they go may best not be left to be settled quietly by a handful of policy analysts in the general system. Instead, the interests of the general system and the developing system will be best served by full and open debate. There can be close examination of population policy, even though it is couched in objective terms of efficiency and economic necessity. And there can be a close watch by the managers on government allotment decisions as agricultural production becomes better managed and output increases.

Lastly, there are further opportunities for development acceleration through close cooperation between agribusiness corporations and farmers' coops.

Managing the Future

What will the development of a viable economic system mean for the future of the United States, and beyond that, how might its impact on the United States affect the rest of the world? It is possible that the kind of development considered here could produce unanticipated consequences with respect to what the country stands for, who its allies are, and how its resources come to be allocated at home and abroad. A thriving Afro-American system at income parity with the general system will mean that the United States will have fundamentally altered one of its most long-standing characteristics.

To speculate briefly on the general direction of those changes, a strong Afro-American component in the American economy and general society may mean that foreign policy will be altered generally and the social debt idea with its orderly redistributive implications may become a factor in the international economy as well as in the domestic. The tendency for U.S. military and aid commitments to buttress those committed to maintaining existing internal distributions of income and wealth ownership, leadership, and participation in the Middle East, in southern Africa, in Southeast Asia, and in the republics of central and south America may be expected to shift in a progressive direction as new leaders with new institutional bases take their places in the policy councils of Cambridge, New York, Washington, and elsewhere. In short, this development may have a moderately liberalizing effect on U.S. domestic and international policy.

How will this development affect government and social relations in the next thrity to fifty years? The study of the future is an expanding field, and the managers of development, especially in the NAA and NUL, can arrange to take systematic, well-organized and institutionalized cognizance of the literature on futurism and the work of the futurists. Indeed, a futures research center, with a small high-quality staff, could be a sound defensive investment against any contrary analysis and planning underway in the futures institutes and think tanks.

5

Constructive Relations With the General Business Community

Following this review of development considerations, it is useful to examine next the participation to be sought from business leadership of the general system. As a practical matter, their active cooperation will be indispensable because of the highly interdependent nature of the society of which Afro America is a subsystem.

A debate has been underway for several years, spurred in part by the leadership of Afro America. Most people know about that debate by now, especially after the well-publicized challenges in stockholders' meetings in the early 1970s. The issue is: What is the general social responsibility of business? And what, if any, role does it have in the development of Afro America?

The answer likely to emerge over the next few years of challenge, study, and compromise is that this responsibility is greater than previously felt by corporate officials but less than many leaders in Afro America would prefer. The business of business is going to turn out to be still the efficient conduct of business, but with an important new dimension.

Some important progressive sectors of business leadership may come to see the broad desirability of somewhat higher effective corporate taxes, fewer tax breaks, and "reordered public priorities"— and this latter phrase really means essentially redistribution of income and wealth. They can recognize that government must deal, often through the private sector, with public issues that no individual firm really can prudently or effectively undertake to handle on a continuing basis.

But first, business leaders with the aid of the development leadership in Afro America can think through some complex and, until recently, taboo questions: Who has been subsidizing whom in the United States? By how much? Has it been equitable? And, if not, what should be done about it to expedite development?

It is reasonable to believe that farsighted business leaders, recognizing the public interest and the desirability of strengthening the

29

developing systems, will agree to some orderly sacrifice, albeit reluctantly.

They will prefer to continue to do what they do best: manage. And they may come to accept explicitly redistributive tax and budget programs, despite the conflict with long-held beliefs. But as yet, they have lacked a suitable rationale for pursuing that course.

There is a school of thought that believes that many aspects of progressive social policy are more readily realized through indirection and tacit agreement. It is felt that explicit consideration of distributive issues, especially if they are also racial, tends to produce unnecessary and avoidable tension, hostility, and generally limited benefits. It is wiser, they believe, to avoid identifying explicitly who will gain and lose in a policy change.

This may be appropriate strategy in some cases. In managing development, however, we are trying not only for concurrence on specific legislation and short-term policy changes, but also a shift in social perception that will influence many aspects of budgetary and procurement policy, in aviation, agriculture, housing , health, trade, transportation, and telecommunications.

So the general public interest and the interests of Afro America would seem to be served by encouraging wide consideration and debate over comprehensive redistributive policy and the social debt rationale.

An alteration of some of the economic beliefs of business leaders is necessary before solid support can be expected for equitable redistribution. To alter those beliefs means that new information, new analysis, must be made broadly available.

The concept of the social debt may be useful in discussing with leaders in the general system ways in which they might assist in development. Most business leaders do not feel guilty about the current effects of slavery and discrimination. And most are not conscious of any material benefits flowing to them collectively from those historical processes. However, they may consider the social debt and support redistributive development programs, once such a debt is established and the concept gains broad public legitimacy. They may then prefer to be consistent with perceived American virtues, among which is the reasonably prompt payment of agreed-upon debts.

So it is partially on the basis of the social debt that long term commitments to support development may be negotiated. There is a social debt. It is often referred to as a moral debt. Perhaps it is ultimately a moral debt, but it is also quantifiable. It is researchable, and statistical techniques enable its magnitude to be estimated in current dollars. It is moral to pay debts once established and agreed upon, and in that sense it is a moral debt. But the point is that it is possible to measure the subsidy from the Afro-American to the general system—and perhaps generally from the have-nots to the haves—through labor and wage discrimination, through discrimination in education, and so on.

There may be initial resistance to the concept and to the implications. But it is reasonable to suppose that as research is completed and made public, the idea, if it stands scrutiny, will gain acceptance. Its policy implications can then be made tangible in the form of redistributive programs based on the taxing power of government at all levels.

What may become clear is that, in a useful sense, money is owed by upper-income groups and corporations—the "Top 20"—to lower-income groups, and from the general system to Afro America. If so, it can help settle the question of relative responsibilities of business and government in support of development.

6

**Managing Redistribution:
The Social Debt**

There is a sketch of a concept of social debt. Partial investigation in an unpublished research project completed at the University of California, Berkeley, has produced estimates of $700 billion for the period 1929–1968.[1] It is useful to consider its implications for managing development.

Historical Perspective

To deal effectively with a range of domestic issues Americans with direct influence on public policy will be more successful if they understand and acknowledge all the sources of current economic conditions. Current conditions are, to varying degrees, the result of discrimination and exploitation of human resources, and most Americans above the income median are the beneficiaries of these processes.

Other Debts

Almost every group in history has at some time exploited another group or been exploited. There could be, in theory, debts all around. But it has not been technically possible to calculate the extent of exploitation and arrange to manage economic redress.

Economic theory, statistical tools, computer capability, and sufficient historical data are available now to permit estimation. And despite its difficulties, the economy of the general American system is strong enough to manage payment without injuring itself.

Afro America can make a serious and supportable claim on the United States because, as a practical matter, it can be negotiated and satisfied. This can be done by the development institutions, the NAA, NUL, NBL, and so on.

What about a Debt to Immigrant European-Americans?

There may be other debts. Further analysis will refine the concept and will focus coverage on those groups and developing systems to which it is appropriate.

There are perhaps many first- or second-generation Americans who, after careful examination, might conclude that they benefit economically from twentieth-century discrimination, especially if their incomes are in the Top 20. They will probably have more difficulty, however, in understanding how they benefit from slavery, and in any case why they are indebted. The reason, put simply, is that virtually free labor in the seventeenth, eighteenth, and early nineteenth centuries provided much of the infrastructure that created the basis for an industrial situation that could welcome immigrants.

Indeed, the present concern of a large portion of the Top 20 over taxes that they believe are being spent to provide too generous benefits to lower-income groups and to developing systems is anomalous when examined in historical perspective. It is reasonable to view slaves as persons who receive marginal-quality to very poor-quality food, clothing, shelter, and medical care and who pay very high income taxes, all of it withheld. Some of the "tax" went to owners, rather than to government, but all the tax went collectively from the Afro-American system to the general system.

What about Debts to Poor Whites and to Other Developing Systems?

Residents of Appalachia and other depressed agricultural, industrial, and mining regions have apparently been victims of the illegitimate transfer of income as a result of industrialization and of general and specific tax, tariff, and agricultural policies, and of a variety of private business practices. These regional income transfers may have affected them as a class. However, they were exploited primarily because they were a vulnerable and relatively immobile labor force. Those who left depressed areas could prosper; those who remained poor were deprived of one of the general advantages of race. In contrast, Afro-Americans of every economic and educational level were discriminated against and exploited because of both class and race, and as a result are disproportionately poor in income and wealth. Clearly, however, all the poor deserve economic stimulation and public policies to aid them. But universalistic language in discussing these matters can be misleading.

A similar technically based debt case can, and in all likelihood will, be made for Indian America, Puerto Rican America, Mexican America, Asian America, and perhaps other developing systems.

Is This an Appeal to Guilt?

Americans in the Top 20 may properly feel guilt for failing to acknowledge an outstanding social debt, but they need not feel non-specific guilt over injustices perpetrated by their ancestors. The second kind of guilt does little good; it cannot help development, and indeed, it can lead to harm through the psychological process called "scapegoating." Americans are not guilty of practicing slavery and most are not currently actively engaged in economic discrimination, but many are collectively the beneficiaries both of slavery and of recent economic discrimination.

A Moral Debt?

If there is a moral issue relevant to the development of public policy on the social debt, it concerns current receipts of a flow of benefits. Slavery is considered by most people—and social discrimination in economic life apparently is considered by many—to be immoral and unjust; the practices have been outlawed, although some economic discrimination continues. The important question remains for many to decide: Is it moral for people to accept collective benefits of admittedly immoral practices, of which they do not approve, but which were committed by their collective ancestors in their behalf? If there is a feeling of guilt about slavery and economic discrimination, development leaders can focus on this issue of current benefits from past and current practices, not simply on the immorality of the practices themselves. This is not an attempt to deal through this social debt concept with noneconomic psychic and cultural effects of past relations. It is not seeking payment for lives lost or damaged.

A Net Debt

It is a net debt. It results from flows of income from accepted or officially sanctioned socially based economic discrimination over 350 years. There have been flows the other way, from the general system through government to Afro America in such forms as housing, welfare, employment, and other development programs. Some who accept the basic argument might nevertheless suppose that the flows cancel one another and that no debt remains. Part of the total income flow perhaps has been paid back in the form of government programs. It should be noted, however, that programs have generally been tolerated by the bulk of taxpayers as a price to be paid to keep people alive, but in their place. The alternative of letting them live wretched totally unproductive lives was considered morally unacceptable, if not economically unfeasible. Those payments, therefore, permitted other attempts at domination—economic, political and cultural—to perpetuate themselves, more or less, until very recently. That is, by accepting tax and budget obligations just sufficient to permit sustenance but hardly any development, the economic arrangements of the 100 year period from Reconstruction to the mid 1960s contributed to a general pattern of social domination with political and economic exclusion from most significant on going activity. The minimum price was paid and development with its resulting economic and political competition was thereby avoided for several generations.

Thus, these payments seem to have been made in the spirit of maintenance for an exploited population that could not effectively be gotten rid of. In the future, only those fiscal cash flows that are constructive and, indeed, developmental, rather than merely subsistence, that contribute to upgrading earning power or provide a basis for personal or community growth and self sufficiency, should be counted toward debt payment. In this category would be programs in quality education and training, home ownership and other quality housing, and in serious economic and business development—all programs that have accounted for relatively few dollars in the past 100 years. Developmental programs could include at least certain portions of a true income maintenance plan or a family assistance allowance designed to set people on their feet and get them moving toward development self-sufficiency, rather than maintain a dominated and underdeveloped system.

Political Realities and Redistribution

The medican income in the United States is around $14, 300, and in Afro America around $8,800. As a practical matter, encouraging public opinion toward income redistribution through progressive taxation to facilitate development probably cannot succeed if it means tax increases for those near the median. The forgotten American, the "silent majority," the Middle 40, has unmet requirements for public goods, as does the Bottom 40. Redistribution through progressive taxation will, therefore, have to begin well above the median and primarily be borne by the Top 20. It will require general tax reform leading to fair and self-enforcing progressive systems.

The concept of social debt can be useful in policy consideration. Until this issue, so far not recognized as profoundly serious, is researched thoroughly, faced squarely, and understood widely, there will probably be continued confusion on policy direction. This is not to say that the treatment of symptoms is unimportant. Quite the contrary. But inadequate diagnosis of the basic problem—illegitimate income transfer and the resulting social debt—tends to hamper effective treatment of symptoms and makes the management of development even more difficult.

It is useful to conceive of policies and programs aimed at correcting urban and social ills as being directed primarily at curbing illegitimate income transfer and transferring income back as debt repayment so as to support the process of development.

Development Objectives and Income Redistribution

It can be helpful to successful development if leaders, managers, and policy analysts can focus on a target of parity in median incomes.

Table 6–1
Trends in Income

	1965	1969	1972	1975	2020
Median family income					
General	6,957	9,433	11,116		say 25,000
Black	3,886	5,999	6,864	8,779	25,000
White	7,251	9,794	11,549	14,268	25,000
Income Gap					
White/Black	3,365	3,795	4,685	5,489	0
Ratio					
Black/White	0.54	0.61	0.59	0.61	1.00

Source: adapted from Andrew J. Brimmer, "Economic Developments in the Black Community," *The Public Interest,* Winter 1974, p. 147.

Note: Current income shares are given in Table 6–2 and may be seen in contrast to the target year 2020 figures.

Table 6–2
Quintile Ranking of Family Shares of Total Income

Families	1950	1970	2020	2050
Bottom 20%	4.5	5.5	10	12.5
Second 20%	12.0	12.0	15	17.5
Third 20%	17.4	17.4	20	20
Fourth 20%	23.5	23.5	23.5	22.5
Top 20%	42.6	41.6	31.5	27.5

Source: adapted from Robert J. Lampman, "What Does It Do for the Poor?—A New Test for National Policy," *The Public Interest,* Winter 1974, p. 72.

They can also work to make the income distributions of the two groups look about the same, although with less dispersion than at present at the high and low extremes.

Currently, median family incomes can be seen from Table 6–1.

By the year 2020 sensible development policies and effective systems management may produce a distribution about as shown in the third column of Table 6–2. This is apparently a more equitable distribution than at present. An equilibrim may be established there or it may be possible to move on to a distribution like that in the fourth column about the year 2050. The problem will be how to get a fair distribution without damaging investment incentives and with-

out penalizing any group unfairly. This is not designed to be puni-
tive. It is intended to produce a distribution like the one that
presumably would exist today had there been an open and fairly
competitive society all along.

Note

1. To be published in *The Social Debt: Policies For Redistributive Justice,* R.F. America, in preparation.

7

Managing the Acquisition of Going Concerns

Development will require that a large number of successful businesses be established and maintained. This process is gaining momentum after a decade of faltering efforts.

A corporate transfer program with federal capital subsidies—employing the important writedown principle—without which acceleration of development will be difficult, is now timely. Housing, health, education, employment, law enforcement, and direct income maintenance are high priorities in efforts to develop. But even with a successful converging of median incomes, a fundamental cause of social dysfunction may remain unless there is sufficient development of institutional strength. In any case, businesses, beginning in their present infant state, probably will not grow fast enough to achieve a development objective of parity by 2020. Major business will still be disproportionately located in the general system. To avoid that outcome, and to achieve parity, a systematic program of transferring large, medium, and small corporations is required. At the outset, small firms in the $3 to $10 million sales range can be emphasized.

A comprehensive development strategy requires a program of subsidized acquisition, as startups will not provide sufficiently broad growth to achieve the development objective.

A program of acquisition depends on ample capital in Afro America. More of this will be available over the next decades, but a program of subsidy for acquisition is justified on the social debt rationale and also because development is in the general public interest.

Program Rationale

The developing system—through the illegitimate income transfer process—has been deprived of an opportunity to save and invest. It

41

therefore has insufficient capital. The assumption here is that sound public policy in support of development can treat this deficiency.

One common objection to this is that it is unfeasible—that no people will, under any circumstances, give over a portion of their wealth, no matter the rationale, and certainly would not yield medium- and large-sized going concerns. Obviously, given an easy choice, virtually any group in a propertied position would be determined not to give it up. Such yielding is likely only if there is a reasonable rationale and sustained political support from the development leaders in Congress, the National Bankers Association, National Urban League, National Association of Black Manufacturers, NAA, National Business League, and the National Economics Association.

Precedents for Transfer

American history does not lack for instances of public resources being used to support private activities when the results were expected to be in the public interest.

An instructive precedent for a transfer mechanism is the urban renewal program. Eminent domain is used for essential public projects, and to change a land use while title to property passes from one private party, through government, to another. The process proceeds after public hearings and with safeguards against abuse, although abuses are not unknown.

The owner is compensated at fair market value for the property, and this payment is from the public treasury. Then property thus acquired is prepared for transfer. Preparation in the case of a new use consists of clearance of structures, preparation of the ground for new construction, and placement of utility lines, street realignments, and curbs. Then the property is sold to the developer, who ordinarily agrees to tenure, use, and design controls, imposed by the developing authority.

The total cost of acquisition and preparation usually far exceeds disposition price to the developer; indeed, it is not uncommon for property to be sold for less than half that total cost. This price, of course, is an even smaller percentage of what a developer might have had to pay to assemble the parcels in the open market without benefit of the public intermediary, assuming the assembly to have been possible at all. The net project costs amount to roughly the difference between total acquisition and the disposition price. The public treasury absorbs the net project cost.

A variation on this mechanism could be employed to accomplish the social transfer of small, medium, and large businesses, or plants or divisions of large companies.

In transfering ownership of corporations, eminent domain would not be a satisfactory method and specifically is not recommended here. The process would require a congenial atmosphere and a high level of cooperation with original owners and managers. Potential obstruction or even sabotage is obvious, so attractive incentives are necessary.

Transfer Mechanism

The process should be initiated by candidates for acquisition. A federal agency facilitating such conveyances would issue a standing invitation to divest. This Agency for Corporate Transfer Act could be set up in the Department of Commerce or independently.

The program could begin with a trial run, one sizeable company transferred in each SBA region, each year for five years. During the five-year test period, the program can be modified to improve the functioning of the subsequent full transfer program.

Two assumptions are implicit: (1) there are sufficient individuals or organizations in Afro America with access to $1 million to $10 million in equity funds to accomplish the private purchase requirement, and (2) there will be sufficient managerial talent to run the transferred concerns. These assumptions are sound enough. Equity money has been found to meet attractive opportunities in the past few years. There is very likely more, but not in sufficient quantity to make write-down subsidies unnecessary. Likewise, the experience of personnel and management recruiting firms in the past five years suggests a pool of management talent. An increasing supply of well-trained business managers and engineers will also be available.

Acquisitions occur in the normal course of business. The ACT mechanism can enable some of this steady turnover to flow to Afro America in an orderly approach to serious government support of business development.

State government can also establish state ACTs. Indeed, in the leading industrial states it might be possible to get an earlier test of this technique than at the federal level. Voluntary transfer requries that the general business system understand its advantages, accept its premises, and concur in its objectves.

Corporate Candidates

Difficulty arises if interest comes largely from marginal firms or those with dim prospects. It might be tempting for a company with management problems, severe and chronic financial or labor problems, obsolescent plant and equipment, or grim marketing problems to seize the opportunity to unload. Rejection because of unsoundness or low potential, however, could cause embarrassment and would tend to discourage seriously troubled companies.

In seeking to develop, competitiveness will be primary. There is little point in transferring many firms in declining industries. On the other hand, those on the technological frontiers like aerospace, ocean industries, and nuclear energy are unlikely to offer themselves. Early transfers are likely to be stable, moderate-growth producers of consumer and industrial goods.

Bidding Procedure

ACT would buy 51 percent of the common stock of acceptable firms. Availability would be made known and offers invited. In the case of a large manufacturer in which controlling interest could be purchased by ACT for $10 million, an acquisition offer of as little as, say, $1 million to $5 million could be sufficient to acquire that interest.

The net acqusition cost—the difference between the price ACT paid for the 51 percent interest and the purchasing group's offer— would be absorbed by the government. The portion of this majority interest not held by these purchasers would be assigned by ACT to a nonprofit organization or a trust of some kind.

Dividends, if any, on these shares would be paid to that corporation and could fund projects in housing, health, training, and so forth. If, however, in management's judgment the interests of the corporation would be best served by retention of earnings, that judgment should not be subordinated to the nonprofit corporation's desire for cash. Funding local public projects in this endeavor is secondary to the goal of sustaining competitive businesses. CDC's and other nonprofit corporations can be more heavily funded directly by government and by the National Fund to accomplish their objectives.

Operations

The period of accomplishing transfer could run one to ten years, depending on size and complexity. How to permit the company to maintain normal operations while the old management is orienting the new? The government can guarantee a rate of return and some negotiated level of sales and net income. This can be done through a government offer to purchase some quantity of product or services, or alternatively through tax concessions.

The former approach is similar in intent to agricultural price supports, which are designed to maintain and protect certain economic activities in the belief that their continuation is in the public interest. Guaranteed markets or returns are also an element in government attempts to stimulate industrial development or investment in developing countries.

Managing Potential Resistance

Negotiations with unions and with all employees in candidate companies can precede transfer, and these groups can have a voice in the decision to transfer. The same can be true for other affected parties, such as financial counselors and bankers, manufacturers' representatives, dealers, suppliers, and principal customers. The involvement of all relevant groups would reduce the risk of direct resistance.

Conclusion

After some reasonable number of transfers have been completed over a twenty- to thrity-year period, the procedure can be discontinued, since by then development momentum can be well established, and economic parity should be within sight of being achieved.

The annual cost of a full program, including administration and profit supports, could be in the range of $1 to $2 billion. A realistic level at the outset might be $100 to $200 million, gradually increasing in scope and funding. The value of the program can rest on the judgment that development will be assisted by a redistribution of existing business institutions.

Manufacturing, transportation, merchandising firms, utilities, banks, and insurance companies can be transferred. In this way, parity can be approached in a reasonable time—that is, in two generations. Other approaches are based implicitly on a policy of gradualism that is insufficiently ambitious. Such policies are limited to efforts to stimulate the growth of small businesses. In time the wisdom of expanded programs can become clear. Most current proposals largely miss the goal of economic parity by 2020.

It can be seen, then, that the transfer program includes a financing technique that can be legislated at any level of government. It does not call for a crash program or for undue and wasteful haste. It contemplates, instead, a deliberate, carefully managed, and prudently funded development program with transfers as the key.

Development leaders and their allies can also consider a related program in which corporate units of all sizes would be transferred involuntarily, using the same write-down financial subsidy. Here, antitrust philosophy can be employed to serve the public interest and to support development by changing the relative economic power concentrations of the general system and the developing systems.

8

Antitrust Innovation and Development

Development leaders and those who analyze related public policy issues can give increased attention to the uses of antitrust and antitrust philosophy. Interracial economic competition can become a focus of policy concern. And antitrust policy can be extended to deal effectively with the racial composition of major markets. The extraordinary degree to which the developing systems are excluded from economic activity is contrary to the public interest in a heterogeneous society like the United States.

Market power per se is the issue, and specifically, the overwhelming degree of market power held in corporate form by a dominant social group in contrast to that in the developing systems. It can be proposed that antitrust reform take racial factors in market composition explicitly into account.

Development managers can work for additional doctrinal bases for an antitrust policy that would take as a concern the creation and maintenance of a sensible level of economic activity in the developing systems and that would equitably inhibit exaggerated levels of economic power in any social group.

It is a complex and politically sensitive issue. But there is an opportunity for development leaders to work to expand antitrust doctrine to cover development concerns. In doing so, the theory of social debt is useful. It is unlikely that American industry would be as socially overconcentrated had there not been systematic illegitimate transfers of income and wealth for 350 years and especially through the last 100 years or so when industrial development has accelerated.

Indications of Development Potential in Antitrust

Awareness of the potential in existing antitrust provisions has been indicated by a Los Angeles suit in which black petroleum retailers,

47

charging price fixing, sought damages in a class action against major distributors of national branded products.

And in October 1971, several organizations, including the NAACP and the Mexican-American Legal Defense and Educational Fund, asked the U.S. Comptroller of the Currency to block the proposed purchase by Wells Fargo Bank of First Western Bank (FWB) unless forty-one FWB branches were sold to developing system and women's groups. These groups charged in their complaint that the takeover would in any case be "anti-competitive," but that if the branches were sold this way, the anticompetitive aspects would be outweighed by the public interest. "Wells Fargo has said it will sell them to a buyer or buyers acceptable to federal banking authorities."[1]

Such use of existing law can become more widespread and more creative. But antitrust reform, while mindful of the negative consequences of overregulation, can go further toward maintaining competition and accelerating development.

Race and Competition

The lack of ownership of large- and medium-sized corporations in the developing systems suggests something inherently racially discriminatory in the structure of major industries. Distortions and denials of equal opportunity in corporate activity at every scale need not be tolerated, given our technical ability to adjust industrial structure.

In order to promote competition, a series of antitrust laws has been created. But competition, because of an apparently inherent bias in market structures, tends to retard the developing systems. It is important, therefore, to alter the racial balance of selected industires to provide a basis for a reasonable degree of competition among social groups. In so doing, the developing systems would have equal opportunities to compete on every scale.

Monopoly by Race

The concept of monopoly, to be useful in this development context, can be modified beyond its usual meaning. Monopoly (1) presents barriers to new participants seeking to enter established fields, (2) impedes innovation, and (3) restricts production. The social "monoly" that can be perceived in the American economy tends to have the same consequences.

Government can deal with monopoly in several ways. It can be passive and hope that monopolists will voluntarily comply. It can break up monopolies and prevent new ones from forming. It can refrain from divestiture and rely on regulation. And last, it can nationalize monopolies.[2]

With respect to social monopoly, the government has apparently chosen the first option, laissez faire, with occasional attempts at the third, regulation. This mix of policies seems inadequate and ineffective. A new emphasis on the second, restructuring, is in order if a development policy is to be pursued and if the maintenance of competition as general policy is to be retained.

However, even with an extension of antitrust thrust, maintaining competition is but one policy, and it will not always be primary.[3] Development requires, however, that competition be given greater weight in policy tradeoffs, though full employment and stable prices remain as primary policy objectives.

Difficulties in Applying Existing Antitrust Law to Encourage Development

It would be difficult to apply antitrust law to racial discrimination in industrial activity. In some minds, there are dangers in stretching any statute or principle designed for one purpose to cover different purposes. According to that view, it would be better to use antitrust as an analogy in developing tools to get at problems of "social monopoly," "social restraint of trade," or "social conspiracy."

A problem in applying antitrust principles to social discrimination is in finding intent or motive. How to show that actions leading to injury were motivated by anticompetitive intent. Defendants could justify actions on seemingly objective grounds, claiming that racial discrimination was not a factor in decisions. So a prevailing antitrust approach concentrating on conduct and intent makes racial discrimination that hampers development difficult to reach.

Concentration on conduct and intent prevents intervention against discrimination institutionalized in normal business policies.

Normal business tends to be exclusionary and, therefore, anticompetitive, but it is difficult to remedy.

The limitations suggest a need for additional tools. Since social discrimination and antidevelopmental behavior have not been a target of antitrust, new policy in that direction would be innovative and bold.

But the Justice Department has been reluctant to move that way. The following dialogue between former Assistant Attorney General Donald Turner and former Senator George Smathers, Chairman of the Senate Committee on Small Business, is instructive in this regard:

Turner: I do not think that it is appropriate for any of us to play God and bring in what I would call social interests, which are, indeed, legitimate interests but cannot be really satisfactorily worked into antitrust law without conferring on someone like me or my superior, the Attorney General, what amounts, I think, to an unsatisfactory degree of discretion.

What I am saying is that it is hard, if not impossible, to approach a merger case, asking the question not only is this anticompetitive, which we do ask, but also wholly apart from competition, is it a good or a bad thing? I don't think it is appropriate for us (the Antitrust Division of the Justice Department) to ask those further questions. I don't think we should.

Smathers: You do not think that somebody should play God. Certainly we should not. On the other hand, the whole purpose of the Antitrust Division is to carry out the *intent* of the Sherman Act and the Clayton Act, and so on. But you do not have the final say, the Supreme Court is there to tell you if you have gone too far in your theory.

Would you not agree that the purpose of the Antitrust Division is to protect the general public and, if it is a close case, it ought to look, should it not, on the side of the general public? If there is any doubt about something being anticompetitive, maybe—not maybe—you should move.[4]

Present law may have wider applicability. The Attorney General and staff exercise considerable discretion in selecting cases. The choice of targets could be influenced by a policy of encouragement of development if development leaders were persuaded that discretionary authority ought to be so used.

Antitrust Law, Racial Bias, and Development

The law of antitrust rests on certain standards of "fair" conduct. These standards of fair business dealings derive from a model of competition in which there are many firms on both the supply and demand sides of a market.

The thrust of antitrust has been to promote competition by making certain conduct illegal. Emphasis has been on acts of business managers that lessen competition. But emphasis on conduct overlooks institutional aspects of economic racial discrimination.

Most business people would deny that their conduct was at fault, citing as causes other factors of commercial social disparity. So standards other than conduct are needed if racially discriminatory barriers to entry are to be lowered.

Kaysen and Turner

A statute proposed in 1959 would rely on market structure rather than on conduct. This would allow a framework in which bias could be incorporated into antitrust policy. Such a policy could be of great consequence for the developing systems.

Kaysen and Turner assert that some market structures, in and of themselves, apart from the conduct of firms, result in either an unacceptable concentration of power or an unacceptable opportunity for abuse. The proposed statute explicitly seeks to curb undue market power, "individually or jointly possessed," subject to the constraint of maintaining desired economic performance.[5]

Present market structures, wherein the largest 2,000 corporations are owned and controlled entirely by one social group, with gross underrepresentation of the developing systems, represents a characteristic or market situation in which a group, a racial group, "jointly" possesses "undue market power." This interpretation offers a serious basis for legislation and for a development-minded policy.

It remains to be determined precisely how social domination of market structures presents a discriminatory high barrier to firms from developing systems. It seems that the prior absence of any large Afro-American corporations tends to discourage subsequent development of any other large firms. Large enterprise is the sole domain of one social group. And it seems that this social structure in the economy makes normal business relations exclusionary in a broad sense and in every major industrial category.

Market structure rather than conduct as a basis for future policy would lead to new remedies. Conduct is subject to injunction; change in structure requires dissolution, divestiture, or divorcement.[6] Thus, of importance to development, the finding of structural fault would result in structural remedies.

So if structures are found to be offensive and harmful to the public interest, a reorganization of the pattern of ownership and control of some major corporations could follow. As a practical matter, a good deal of habit—a tendency towards reluctance and administrative inertia—might arise to block the use of new statutory authorization for restructuring industries to contribute to development.

Development leaders can consider Kaysen and Turner's proposal and its potential for producing a more competitive and equitable economy.

Incorporating Race Discrimination into Kaysen and Turner

Section 1 establishes the position of the statute: unreasonable market power injures trade and commerce. Such power can be held by any person or group. For the purpose of reducing excessive social barriers, the "group" considered would be the several racial groups, or as defined in this context, the general system and the developing systems.

Although in the Kaysen and Turner framework, the "group" referred to is some combination of firms in a given market, the definition of "group" could be extended to include any racial group. Unreasonable market power, held by *any* group in any combination of markets, is deemed illegal. Given this criterion, it is reasonable to include as illegal a grossly disproportionate dominance by any racial group in industrial categories such as network television, most manufacturing, banking, retailing, and so on.

Next, Section 2 defines market power and presents a standard by which to judge "unreasonble" market power. Group market power would be established by examining performance results. If, without justification, ownership patterns in any market do not reflect broad social composition, then the market is overly concentrated. Some group is then found in possession of unreasonable or unacceptable market power.

In determining whether a racial group possesses market power which in itself is harmful to competition, the major variable would be its ownership control in the industry. This would require the computation of racial concentration ratios.

Excessive dominance by any group works to the systematic detriment of other groups by presenting to them an unfairly high barrier to entry. Such developing groups are thus deprived of equal economic opportunity, and redress would be sought by reorganization. So in addition to the performance variables suggested by Kaysen and Turner, another can be added to prove unreasonable market power: namely, failure of developing systems to attain a reasonable level of ownership and control in any industrial category under investigation. This suggests reorganization where practicable if there is a gross absence of participation.

The social percentage participations finally deemed unacceptable for each industry are complex issues to be decided through research and the legislative process. They are to be decided in each industry through analysis, debate, and bargaining. They cannot be simply quotas based on population share.

Unreasonable exclusion resulting from unreasonable market power by any racial group can be presumed when a developing system enjoys a market share less than a target share established after analysis of that industry.

For example, look at banking. It may be determined after study that Afro-American banks should account for, say, 8 percent of all assets in the banking industry. At present, such banks hold in the aggregate less than one percent of such assets.

A look at technical and economic realities may suggest that through reorganization that share could be brought to 8 percent over, say, a twenty-five-year period. If there has been illegal structural discrimination, structural remedies would be applied to bring the industry into compliance. Over a period of years, orderly reorganization would bring that share into the range of 8 percent. The percentage target chosen would take cognizance of practical realities in reorganization. The same can be done with other industries such as chemicals and drugs, iron and steel, electrical machinery, and so on.

This process of careful reorganization might not result in economic parity by a target date, but it can aim for a level of reorganization that will reduce to insignificance discriminatory barriers to entry. This is a minimum requirement, and it can greatly help development.

Explicit concern for development allows any developing system redress if denied an equal opportunity to compete, as judged by observed representation in industrial structure. It is similar to guarantees of equal rights under law, or one person, one vote; in this case, a right to carry on major industrial activity. Absence from an industry would be prima facie proof of an unfair disadvantage. If intentional efforts by existing firms cannot be found to have caused the absence, then it can be concluded that market structure is at fault and needs alteration. Obviously, in some industries no remedy will be practical for a very long time but in many, timely and straightforward corrections will be possible.

Kaysen and Turner find justifications for certain forms of monopolistic performance, but there is no justification for handicapping any group in its efforts to develop. Given that certain market situations are, under this concept, illegal, how shall structure be changed? Kaysen and Turner propose a special Economic Court to consider reorganization of offending structures.

It would be convenient in reorganizing to accord with parity to require that firms or segments of firms ordered to divest be first offered, where feasible, to an ACT that would have first option to purchase the separated units. This sell-off option would be ordered by the Economic Court, keeping in mind aggregate social compositions of specified industrial categories. So if the court finds imbalance, it can order divested companies for sale on option to the Agency for Corporate Transfer. This technique would facilitate transfers to accomplish the objective of supporting development. At the outset, as a practical matter, proceedings could be limited to those industries where excessive market power is most obvious and where structural reform is most feasible.

Kaysen and Turner suggested that the statute prohibit divestiture where it can be shown that new concerns resulting would lack reasonable prospects for survival. So because of a shortage of capital or managers, or for other practical reasons, social divestiture may for a time be precluded in industries where it is clearly warranted. However, as earlier urged, on the infant industry analogy, such transferred firms can be subsidized for a reasonable period to insure them a fighting chance.

Conclusion

In seeking causes for the absence of large corporations in the developing systems, overt discrimination is insufficient as an explanation. Corporations have grown despite predatory tactics by dominant firms. But there are almost none in the developing systems. Also, most forms of overt market actions that are discriminatory are covered by existing law. So what has stymied development of large firms in the developing systems? The most persuasive explanation is simply the existence of social patterns of ownership, i.e., market structures that present, in and of themselves, discriminatory and high barriers. Other phenomena have also restrained development. But even given these factors, it is reasonable to suppose that large corporations would have developed.

Something like a rule of reason can be applied in extending antitrust assumptions and policies to bring about a degree of "workable interracial competition" in the general American economy.

In 1972 a bill to create an Industrial Reorganization Commission and an Industrial Reorganization Court was introduced in the U.S. Senate and referred to the Judiciary Committee. Its thrust follows the Kaysen-Turner statute. The bill—the Industrial Reorganization Act—has been revised and reintroduced and deserves attention from development leaders.

Notes

1. *San Francisco Chronicle,* October 27, 1971, p. 31.

2. Claire Wilcox, *Public Policies Toward Business* (Irwin, 1960), p. 49.

3. Ibid., p. 335.

4. *Hearings before the Senate Committee on Small Business, Status and Future of Small Business,* Part 2, Ninetieth Congress, March, April 1967, p. 747.

5. Carl Kaysen and Donald F. Turner, *Antitrust Policy* (Cambridge, Mass.: Harvard University Press, 1959), p. 58.

6. Ibid., p. 59.

9

Crime Impedes Development

Afro America has a leadership group that is heavily responsible for progress toward development. It is apparent that crime and other misbehavior are impediments to development. They produce fear among customers of random attack in public and this has as a consequence altered retail shopping patterns and restricted recreation and entertainment decisions with negative impact on those industries. It raises insurance and property protection costs, and it creates a general climate of distrust and personal suspicion, hostility, and non-cooperation that undermines attempts at coordinated economic and business development.

It may turn out that mass media, consumer motivation research, and marketing techniques will permit leaders to succeed in managing crime.

Furthermore, although government responses and support from foundations and business are important, the development organizations may turn out to be of greatest consequence in managing crime. Managerial and developmental perspectives will permit development leaders and other analysts to consider proposals concerning crime and its relationship to community development from a more functional point of view. Rather than a legalistic, social welfare, or moralistic attitude, a managerial point of view may be most useful in bringing about a sense of order and compliance with law.

A Development Perspective

For ten years, leaders and opinion makers in Afro America have appeared confused and ambivalent about an appropriate stance on crime. The dominant tone has been that crime is principally a function of harsh, unfair, or oppressive social and economic arrangements. The implication has been that policies that treat causes of crime would reduce it.

57

This has been widely assumed and accepted. And it persists in many quarters. And it is probably true that comprehensive well-designed, well-managed social reforms and community development programs would substantially reduce criminal activity. However, such efforts are being delayed for complex reasons. In the meantime, during this delay, it remains desirable that crime be more effectively managed. So by the mid-1970s, there arose a new attitude: crime can be dealt with in the near term even while reforms to deal with both presumed and demonstrated causes are delayed by political and economic realities.

Even with emerging intolerance, however, confusion lingers about both how to deal with criminality and about a suitable rationale for a firm policy on it. Some of this residual softness appears to derive from a shortage of information on policy choices and consequences and also from failure to consider the issue in the context of general system development.

Crime is an impediment to development. This consideration can help in finding strategies to combat criminals. Until the dysfunctional effect of crime on development is widely appreciated, however, there will continue to be equivocation and procrastination.

The Role of Leadership

In getting to full development and to income and wealth parity, the leaders of major organizations such as the National Association for the Advancement of Colored People and the National Urban League are key. As earlier noted, these organizations may better be conceived of as development rather than as civil rights organizations. And their leadership may more appropriately be drawn from managerial or policy analytic pools than from civil rights, journalism, social welfare, legal or religious backgrounds, as in the past.

Other organizations can also help. The National Business League is potentially important in managing crime. In addition, CORE, SCLC, and PUSH could play worthwhile roles. These have had varying emphases over the last several years, and for complex reasons have exerted only limited influence in development. But the potential of each, given managerial leadership, functional structure, and adequate and reliable resource bases, is high.

Organizational identity can influence effectiveness, and identity can be heavily shaped by names. PUSH, for example, may be handicapped by a name that may detract from credibility. People United to Save Humanity might be usefully changed to, say, Programs Uniting Skill and Heart, or Progress Using Strength and Honor. The acronym is valuable, but the name may be a source of subtle handicap.

Likewise, the NAACP, venerable leader of development efforts, might be more effective as simply NAA, National Association for Advancement. Many have always called it the NAA or "N Double A," so such a change should not be traumatic. Fraternal, social, religious, and professional organizations are also important to development, and as they learn to perceive themselves as having development roles, acceleration toward development will be aided.

In some respects, it is as important who the leaders of development organizations are as who the elected leaders of the general system are. In some ways it is as important who are leading the NUL and the NAA and, to a lesser extent, NBL, CORE, SCLC and PUSH, as who are leading the nation. Their skill, wisdom, energy, example, and analytical power can greatly influence development. And, to the contrary, their incapacity for whatever reasons, can impose great opportunity costs on Afro America. Indeed, those jobs are so important that they deserve what they have not received—regular, external, impartial, and serious scrutiny and criticism. Journalists and other responsible analysts can pay attention to the performance of these institutions and leaders as they do to governmental bodies and elected and key appointed officials. This process might begin with the issue of crime and its impact on development.

In early 1976, Vernon Jordan, Executive Director of the National Urban League, appeared before the Congressional Joint Economic Committee to offer remarks on employment policy. He spoke of the need for a comprehensive set of policies to stimulate and maintain full employment. In commenting on the government's tolerance of the 7 percent unemployment rates of the 1975–76 period, he mentioned as consequences "hidden social costs and unbearable personal costs." "One such hidden cost," he said, "is crime." "Earlier this week," he went on, "the *New York Times* headlined a page one story, 'Crime Rose in Richer Neighborhoods.' Now this does not mean that rich folk have taken to burglarizing their neighbors. It means that people who are poor, who are out of work, who see no prospects, will find any means to survive, even if it means breaking laws. If you do not offer a man productive employment and self-respect and the opportunity to earn his way, he will seize whatever means are available to him, regardless of legality. There is a direct correlation between joblessness, especially teenage unemployment, poverty, and other forms of economic deprivation and the rising crime rate."

There may be such a correlation. There probably is even a causal relation. But it is also probably true that it is possible to reduce sharply and permanently limit crime even during periods of general economic difficulty. In any event, there seems to be a tendency for development leaders to attempt to offer a tradeoff, as if it were negotiable; reduced crime in exchange for various kinds of progressive public policies. Crime is an impediment to development, and it need not be tolerated on any rationale even for short periods. The tendency to explain it in terms of macroeconomic phenomena may even exacerbate the problem by making it seem almost excusable.

Poverty and employment deficiencies deserve continuing attention. These economic problems, however, need not lead to community disorganization, fear, and hostility.

Beyond muggings, burglary, rape, murder and other types of personal assault, vandalism and graffiti are also crimes that hinder development. Furthermore, gang activity is crime. Referring to it as "the gang problem," as many journalists and politicians do, is not helpful. This is a misleading euphemism and tends to make it appear to be something less than criminal.

Some leaders, as noted, apparently believe that they can somehow use crime and disorder as bargaining elements. They have implied, from time to time, that if social and developmental programs are fully supported and fully funded, then crime will be ended more or less. And they have further implied that somehow they could reduce crime quickly in return for some kind of commitment from government. So crime for some has been politicized in this way and remains, as in the 1960s, a kind of political statement.

If there ever were any validity to such a position, it has eroded now. Development is now the principal concern and crime is increasingly seen as retarding development and tending to undermine the confidence and trust of individuals and institutions. Those who imply that crime can somehow be bargained away are pretending to have leverage that they do not have.

Even in the political and governmental climate of the mid-1970s, it is likely that general urban crime can be reduced greatly. It would be easier if key elected officials had the moral stature to lead by example and direction. There appears to be a deficiency on this dimension, which may explain in part why there has been such lethargy on the problem. But key public figures in the general society, as well as in Afro America, are the ones to give initial momentum to a return to self-discipline, even in the face of hard times and lingering resentment from social and political conflicts of the 1960s.

Most people know right from wrong, and so do most criminals. A series of communications from elected officials and respected development leaders may be required to bring about some rethinking. The means of communication could be electronic, written, and face-to-face. A series of fireside chats, perhaps, in which behavioral expectations are explained and in which audiences are reminded of standards of personal conduct in a complex multicultural society may be one important ingredient in a strategy of behavioral reform. Such approaches, if well conceived and well executed, need not be condescending, threatening, or patronizing. Just straight talk about serious issues may be enough. A national campaign, and private and public local campaigns may be required.

It may be discovered that there are no leaders or combinations of leaders and social marketing techniques, local or national, who have sufficient stature to influence mass behavior in the short run, by words, no matter how skillfully or how genuinely presented. If so, we would have learned an important lesson about the limits of leadership and about the limits of communications.

The assumption with this specific element in a crime control program is that the criminal and potential criminal audience hasn't been told by the right people in the right way to straighten up. It is well known that such simple but important direct communication can be sufficient to correct certain types of behavior. It appears that this has not been tried with this mass phenomenon of urban violent crime and related nuisance behavior.

At the same time, reality requires that serious and high probability penalties for those who persist can follow. A credible threat of punishment, for example, imprisonment and loss of freedom for the few, can accompany leadership for the many.

It is a good guess that crime will persist at high levels until the development leadership perceives that it is a high priority matter, a threat to long-term development, and deserves direct sustained action without equivocation. Many see law and order and crime in the streets as racial supremacist code words left over from 1968 and 1972. To some extent, they are right. Despite that, however, both the general welfare and specific development require that over the next several years, crime be treated as a priority issue.

Contributing Factors

A long list of social elements can be cited as contributing historically to bringing about the problem of crime in the 1970s. The roots lie in economic exploitation in the seventeenth, eighteenth, and nineteenth centuries. The trail would lead on through hostile public policies following the Civil War and on into the twentieth century. The Depression, displacements caused by World War II, and subsequent internal migrations on a large scale from rural to urban settings all contributed to stressful conditions.

In the last two decades a dozen elements would bear mention. The Civil Rights Movement and civil disobedience; the antiwar movement and the Vietnam War itself, the Community Control and Black Power movements, the New Left and some aspects of popular Marxist social analysis, police brutality and the response to it, law and order and support your local police movements, unemployment, the War on Poverty, Maximum Feasible Participation, drugs, permissiveness, and the counter culture, the sexual revolution, rock and roll, television, the women's movement, the white backlash, the prohibition of religion in the schools, Watergate, assassinations, exploitation films, and general moral shifts.

Managing Crime

A serious analysis of crime in the late 1970s focusing on any one of these elements as a principal contributor is possible. But none of it excuses the problem. Despite all that, crime can be managed. An ethical basis for community life, even in the face of serious structural economic dislocation, can be restored. And individual and family morality and responsibility can be rediscovered and at least partially restored in areas where it has diminished. It is the task of the leadership to develop strategy and programs using internally generated private resources together with government grants and corporate cooperation to manage effectively crime throughout the developing system.

The practical need for right conduct has been a theme from Richard Allen through Douglass, DuBois, Washington, King, Young, Wilkins, and Jackson. The dominant harsh public policy toward crime in the South after the Civil War has undoubtedly contributed to the attitudes of some black people toward law and authority even to the present day. In addition to the injustice in the criminal justice system at the time, the economic exploitation built into that system through the leased convict labor process has apparently contributed to general disrespect as well as to contemporary economic inequality. But even having recognized these issues, there is no justification in any of this history for current disorder and lawlessness.

Taking the Policy Initiative

What will be done in response to crime need not be reactionary in spirit if the leadership can take the initiative. They can do this not merely to preempt the law and order reactionaries in the general system, but rather because it makes sense for them to lead in solving this problem and it fits a developmental strategy.

There has been some tendency in the early and mid-1970s for policy commentators in the general media and in the influential press to forget that the general system retains many serious elements of social injustice. But inequity and racism notwithstanding, development is the objective, and crime is an impediment and can be managed and reduced. This can be done although injustices persist.

The criminal law represents, on the one hand, say some expert observers, the agreement by high-status groups in any society to label certain behavior and certain people as deviant and outsiders. But the law also expresses a general reasoned broad social consensus, especially as it concerns violent and predatory crime. These orderly values transcend the immediate and political interests of individuals and groups.

This reality helps to undermine the tendency by some to equivocate on policy responses to urban violent crime. There is virtually unanimous social disapproval of this criminal phenomenon, and apologists for criminals cannot expect to prevail against this social force. Afro America's views on what is crime, especially on what kinds of assaultive behavior are criminal, are not at odds with the general American view.

Many commentators also habitually balance violent crime off against white-collar business crime. This tendency leads to a kind of personal intellectual stalemate in which it is made to appear unjust to deal with lower-class young criminals before an equally effective campaign is undertaken with upper-middle- and upper-class older criminals. Development requires that this conceptual stalemate be broken. Measures can be taken in the short run that are technically possible and politically feasible to deal with urban violent crime, even while working for a more difficult formation of consensus or coalition to proceed on economic or so-called upper-world crime.

Order Despite Low Incomes

Law enforcement and order are important because they serve developmental interests. But they are also matters of social value. The principal policy support for a firm approach to crime is that a set of strategic and broadly beneficial Afro American interests will be served by a reduction in crime and in its associated individual and institutional insecurities.

Urban violent crime probably can be traced in part to "extremist" sentiment of the 1965–1972 era. That sentiment has not entirely been dissipated, so a policy of determined law enforcement and stable community order can take account of the persistent view in some quarters that crime is somehow a legitimate political expression and a response to oppression.

Since the 1970s crime seems historically related to the 1960s' rebellions, it is worth considering whether removing the apparent "causes" of crime would very likely be any more effective in insuring domestic tranquility than was the attempt at removing what were believed to be the causes of riots. The answer, is, probably no—no more effective. Direct and firm law enforcement, together with sophisticated social marketing and communication, is very likely going to turn out to be the preferred course. The reason for undertaking development, after all, is that developmental gains are desirable for their own sake. Order and community harmony is a precondition of development rather than a result of it.

Criminal Motivation and the Attractiveness of Crime

A great deal of technical analysis of crime and of public policy toward crime is available in the specialized literature. But the principle of attempting to manage the perceived costs and benefits of crime to the potential criminal by affecting the perceived risks and penalties, so as to gain greater popular compliance with law, is really only common sense.

Urban Violent Crime (UVC) may have reached the levels it has in the 1970s because, among other reasons, there has been insufficient quality information urging compliance with the law broadcast to the potential criminal social groups.

If low-income, young males are the principal population group in question, then they may have been inclined to this criminal behavior, in part, because they have been, in effect, isolated from those in the population who define crime unfavorably. To correct this situation of social isolation requires, then, that they be reached by a steady and effective stream of communications urging and directing compliance.

It is the duty of the leadership in Afro America and in the general system to arrange to break this pattern of isolation and to secure compliance through imaginative and effective communication. In this way, the weight of favorable definitions of crime coming to them from peers may be exceeded by the weight of unfavorable definitions coming to them from impersonal sources through the media. The values of the larger system, in these matters of compliance with the law, may come to outweigh those of the peer group. Indeed, through the use of the media, the peer groups' attitudes as well toward compliance with law, and even perhaps towards general morality, may be changed.

It has also been suggested that healthy small business and commercial development will tend to depress crime and will help reduce the attractiveness of crime in target neighborhoods. But since crime impedes development, it is probably necessary to find first such independent enforcement and communication measures as suggested here, or others, for managing crime, before commercial life can really be expected to flourish.

Even in the face of continued discrimination, dual labor markets, restricted mobility, and other such impediments to immediate self-improvement, increased crime need not result if countervailing programs aimed at reinforcing high-level values, attitudes, morality, and community spirit are undertaken to change the attractiveness of crime.

Managing crime successfully also requires that semantic adjustments be made to attain a higher degree of clarity in policy debate and in the formation of broad public opinion. "Juvenile delinquency," for example, is crime for the most part, and the interests of community order and development are perhaps best served by dropping euphemisms such as "vandalism," "the gang problem," "juvenile delinquency," and so on.

The sustained public information campaign that will be necessary to help manage the attractiveness of crime can be one that uses words like crime and criminals, where appropriate, without equivocation, unless it can be clearly demonstrated that softer language is more functional in changing the taste for crime and undisciplined behavior.

Unease

In city after city, many people responding to professional surveys say they feel unsafe. "Many," as a practical matter, may be defined as low as, say, 10 percent. It is a good guess that if as many as 10 percent of adult citizens feel unsafe, they will learn to behave in defensive and uncooperative ways that are dysfunctional from a developmental point of view. Their shopping and recreational and investment habits will be altered just enough to make the difference between thriving local retail districts, for example, and marginal or submarginal ones.

In some cities black unease is found to be high, at over 10 percent and in several, quite high, at over 20 percent. Development may be presumed to be retarded when such a large proportion of the population feels unsafe and untrustful of their fellows in random public contact.

School Crime

Crime in the schools is clearly a threat to development, as it undermines processes of education and human capital formation. Viewed this way, a stronger consensus in support of firmness and order in urban schools may be generated.

A commitment to expulsion, difficult to implement though many believe it to be, may be a necessary policy. It is generally assumed that there would be a wholesale exodus, and that therefore no such separation of chronically troublesome people would be feasible. Here again, the key may be the sophisticated use of the media, together with a systemwide commitment to fundamental educational effectiveness and basic skill development.

The principal development organizations, the NUL and NAA, have a leadership role to play to eliminate crime in the schools. They can work effectively with police and school administrators in beaming a determined message to the intended groups that schools will be safe and even pleasant places in which to study.

Vandalism and Graffiti

Vandalism and graffiti are serious collective crimes. They have received little effective attention from the development leadership, which appears to view them as trivial or merely annoying. This behavior tends to undermine community self-respect and cohesion and deserves to be dealt with strictly and consistently.

Education and publicity, deterrence and retribution can all be included as elements in a social marketing program. The question to be asked is how to manage small property crime, i.e., vandalism, and how can publicity be designed to have maximum effect?

The philosophical questions of how much control is acceptable in a democracy and of what is vandalism symbolic can be helpful in designing an effective program to stop it. But they need not be pondered in quest of a basic decision as to whether to take forceful action.

Managerial Responses to Crime

Does punishment deter crime? Some experts believe that the frequency with which a given punishment is applied is of greater importance than its severity. But what is the role of information in managing crime and in getting out the word on the likelihood of punishment?

Development organizations can systematically improve the crimnal audience's understanding of the probabilities of the several sets of consequences through social marketing. Getting these risks across, as has been noted, would be an important component of a well-conceived program of community information. It may be that a steady program of such information, not threatening—just giving the facts—could produce substantial behavior changes. Crime seems to occur in part because "criminals are not very well informed" about the severity and frequency of punishment. This is a subject of debate, with some observers feeling that crime occurs in part because criminals are, indeed, well informed about the low probabilities of serious consequences. No doubt some are well informed and know that in some jurisdictions the consequences at law are not appropriately severe or frequent. As those realities change in favor of strong deterrence, potential criminals can be better informed.

Indeed, the press in Afro America and perhaps particularly the major periodicals, together with the National Newspaper Publishers Association, have an opportunity to review their policies on reporting and featuring crime stories. Their contribution to crime by way of their past and present practices is a fit subject for analysis. And their potential role in bringing down crime and enhancing development can likewise be examined in this context.

The taste both of the criminal for crime and of other citizens for conformity is of great importance. So the question for the leadership is how to influence those tastes in such a way as to cause desirable changes in behavior. Social marketing is the general solution, and the specific program is that the leadership design and implement a campaign aimed at behavior modifications in both criminals and in law-abiding citizens.

Crime and Trust

Sustained levels of personal trust and even feelings of affection for
the immediate local community and for Afro America are necessary
if there is to be development. This is so because development will
require a broad readiness to make some sacrifices in money—contributions to political and general welfare funds—and in time and
energy to community projects and improvement campaigns. Unless
large numbers of people are inclined to make such occasional
sacrifices on behalf of collective progress and to accept some inconvenience and place some trust in strangers, there will be no development. Such "public regarding" and "other regarding" attitudes are
a prerequisite for successful development.

Crime tends to undermine trust and in that way hampers development. It may have a more damaging economic impact through its
erosion of trust even than in its direct harm done to individuals and
enterprises.

The Criminal Justice System

A comprehensive strategy for manging crime requires a thoughtful
policy on prisons and other institutions for holding the convicted.
Some who have studied the issue doubt that massive investments in
new prison structures and institutional programs will do what is expected—reduce crime and rehabilitate criminals.

Corrections programs have tended not to be as effective as
expected. The reasons are probably similar to those that explain the
general failure of certain other social programs: insufficient scale and
resources, sabotage by administrators privately hostile to the program or the concept, incompetent management, a hostile press, as
well as real conceptual inadequacies. In addition, there has been no
effective social marketing program concurrent with the corrections
effort. Without such a sophisticated public information program, no
aspect of the criminal justice process will realize its full impact on
the behavior of potential criminals.

It is also important that the development leadership encourage
rehabilitative programs in prisons and on the outside as well. There
is, of course, a great deal of outspoken skepticism about the possibility of rehabilitation on any significant scale. Some of this doubt is

registered by those who are hostile to development in any dimension, some by those who are fiscal conservatives legitimately concerned about expensive programs, and some by people who have made respectably thorough examinations of existing programs and found that they are ineffective for a complex set of reasons.

Urban Violent Crime

The principal focus of concern, the kind of behavior that appears to be most destructive of the mutual confidence and respect needed for development, is violent predatory crime.

One reason for violent crime and disorder is that traditional interpersonal sanctions have been frozen, often by fear of retaliation, often by indifference. They need to be restimulated. So development organizations can campaign to reinforce basic standards of fit conduct.

The NUL and NAA and other development institutions have a direct information role to play in speaking to the criminal and potential criminal population. They also have a responsibility to conduct a program aimed at the general community and to the pool of potential victims of UVC.

The campaigns can "harden the targets" and thereby serve to control crime from the victim's side. Somehow this should be done in a manner that does not generate high levels of cynicism and mistrust among the general population but instead encourages alertness and personal responsibility. Some observers have noted a tendency toward verbalized justifications for law violations by survey respondents in Afro America. These explanations are rationalizations based on a general feeling of gross systemic injustice.

A program attempting broad-based attitude change using a mix of media and marketing techniques can take account of these rationalizations, and messages can be designed to offset such views and replace them with more forward-looking and developmental attitudes. One reason that violent criminal conduct follows these feelings of injustice is the relative absence of countervailing messages.

Focusing on motives may prove to be helpful in understanding crime. And it may be even more useful in helping to manage it. Research has found that across demographic categories and across ideological categories, black people "agreed that it was not okay" to break the law "even if they were not caught." This is very important. This must be the overwhelming sentiment if development is to proceed, and it must prevail and be reinforced through communications over any justifications based on historic injustice.

Police Performance

The inferences that can be drawn from data on the effect of more police and more patrols on crime and crime rates are highly debatable, such is the complexity of the subject. But the level of patrol is an important consideration for those concerned with development and community order.

It is often claimed that police treatment of young black people is consistently biased and unfair, even illegal. There is a widespread feeling that police practice has been "oppressive" and that crime in the mid-1970s can be partially traced to police abuses and police "brutality" in the 1950s and 1960s.

Development and effective law enforcement would seem to depend on firm and fair police practice. Development organizations can pay attention to the behavior and attitudes of law enforcement leadership and rank-and-file officers. However, they also can avoid dwelling on these issues, as was the habit in the 1960s. Excessive and especially emotional concern for these factors seems to undermine community order and encourage both lawlessness and cynical attitudes toward high standards of behavior. It is important, therefore, that the leadership monitor police practices in a consistent manner and establish private formal mechanisms for seeking reform and correction of abuses when they are observed.

The purpose of police activity and of the entire criminal justice system is to contribute to a condition of general compliance with the law and of stable community order. This is a desirable condition because order is intrinsically preferable to disorder and also because it is conducive to creativity, production, development, and individual fulfillment for the great majority of citizens. Those who need some greater degree of disorder to satisfy an idiosyncratic aesthetic or social taste can find communities that are suitable. Most communities will be best served by order and by a high level of voluntary compliance with the law.

Other potentially useful instruments in managing crime are the various associations of black police officers. They may be in especially key positions to aid in the development of communitywide respect for law and personal self control if they come to perceive themselves as instruments in a development process. ·

The development leadership can make it a point to establish contact with organizations such as the Afro American Patrolman's League. Indeed, a comprehensive program of law enforcement and community order requires that development agencies and police organizations of all kinds maintain a harmony of purposes and approaches.

The thrust of this discussion of crime fits the general theme and emphasizes developmental imperatives rather than any real or imagined historical justifications for crime, disorder, or individual noncompliance with universally understood norms of public behavior.

The idea that high-crime groups in a developing system are simply reacting to their circumstances is not very helpful for purposes of guiding policy thinking. Effective management of criminality, as an essential to development, can remain a priority objective and can prevail against a variety of popular but nonpragmatic social science conclusions about criminal motivation.

It is likely that perceptive leadership and intelligent use of the media can counter, and at least partially affect, such forces as anomie, alienation, and frustration that, no doubt, do contribute to criminality if unattended in any way.

The development leadership can also decide that it has responsibilities to focus on interpersonal and collective integrity. The level of integrity can be addressed by the leadership just as can the problem of simple criminality. Government will not fill the void to remedy any deficiencies in personal honor, but the development organizations can find ways to address this delicate issue.

Bribery, for example, is a source of development friction in many traditional settings, and it may become a potential source of difficulty here. The temptation to bribe and to seek bribes exists in the United States and in the business development processes in all communities. One reason for seeking a deep commitment to compliance with law and moral behavior for the population at large is that creeping corruption in business and government administration can make the development process demoralizing and grossly unfair to most of the people. Establishing a concern for morality and ethical practice can make the development process a legitimate and open matter unburdened by an Afro-American equivalent of "dash" or payoffs for licenses, permits, contracts, and the like.

Social Marketing

Social marketing is an approach to crime management that can become a key element in development. It is a program that the NUL, NAA, PUSH, SCLC, CORE, and NBL can use to bring about a return to stable and orderly communities. The job could be difficult if it were to involve a great deal of reconditioning. But a key assumption is this—the vast majority of people know right from wrong, and would prefer to do right. In fact, most do right even under some very difficult circumstances. But even those whose lives are somewhat disorganized share enough of the basic social values of honesty, self discipline, and generally lawful conduct so that a program designed to produce high and uniform standards of behavior would not face great barriers.

Each of the market segments in Afro America has a stake of some kind in law enforcement and community order and stability. A marketing program would be designed to persuade, direct, or lead criminals and potential criminals to refrain from crime. Another aspect would seek the support of the remainder of the community for policies and programs of law enforcement and the maintenance of order.

Shoplifting is an essentially subversive and frequent crime, and its antidevelopmental character is clear. Strong measures to bring it to very low levels will be widely supported, and the leadership can make such a campaign a high-priority matter and can expect some support if it is carefully designed and managed. Whether changes in behavior would actually be deep, wide, and lasting would depend greatly on the characteristics of the campaign rather than on any inherent characteristics of the populations.

Graffiti, Discourtesy, Dishonesty, Littering, and Profanity

In addition to actual crime, certain other behavior seems to impede development and to subvert community order. Rudeness in both private and public relations, dishonesty in personal dealings, litter, public uncleanliness, and profanity are in that category. All these may be subject to improvement through social marketing.

There is an almost reflexive use of certain four-letter and four-syllable words in many communities, especially by people under thirty years old. This practice is probably both harmful and correctable. Obscenity, public and private, is destructive. Profanity appears to undermine trust and makes cooperative behavior more difficult. It threatens the authority of the leadership, both elected and private, and deserves to be seen for what it is, an undisciplined and counterproductive habit.

How to provide moral leadership in the public educational system, as well as through the private programs of the NAA, NUL, SCLC, NBL, CORE, and PUSH, seeking to produce a satisfactory level of moral awareness, while avoiding manipulation and indoctrination, will require careful thought. Character training will remain a primary responsibility of family and adult relatives and neighbors, but institutional programs, including social marketing, will be important supplements.

Development requires some increased ethical standard in at least some sectors of the population. Education for self-discipline, respect for legitimate authority, and a high individual value placed on justice in dealings can be pursued using both public and private resources. However, the techniques that will make social marketing most effective in producing short-run behavior and attitude changes may be controversial, i.e., they may be seen as indoctrination.

Noncriminal offenses are of great importance in setting the tone of day-to-day life in the community. Loitering, loud playing of radios, smoking in public places and on transportation, vulgarity and profanity, littering, minor traffic violations, all undermine respect and cohesion and are to be discouraged and, where appropriate, punished. It may be that the financial straits of many big cities—notably, of course, New York in the mid-1970s—would be greatly relieved by much greater self-discipline by average citizens in the matter of trash and garbage disposal and minor traffic infractions, not to mention in educational and in residential property maintenance.

Some observers believe that the "ghetto" is an overwhelming force that can take away the rational ability to perceive an individual stake in obeying the law. Such forces exist, but they can be offset by concerted leadership effort. The key operating assumption can remain that the majority of criminals and potential criminals know right from wrong, and simply take the path of least resistance for a variety of reasons, none of which are acceptable as excuses.

Enunciating the law through the mass media will contribute to the prevention of infraction. And spelling out the actual legal consequences in a well-designed public program can also be expected to be salutory. Communication is a key element in managing crime. There are numerous behavioral issues that can be brought continuously to the attention of the mass audience.

Planning for the Future of Crime

There is a need for forthright discussion of behavioral genetics and of neurophysiological issues in the context of the policy debate on crime. Development organizations can lead the way. These cannot be taboo subjects. They are obviously loaded and subject to ideological distortion and abuse. But there is going to be research on these matters, and the leadership, rather than seeking to discredit it as racially motivated—though some of it is—can be helpful by participating and influencing the direction and spirit of research and the manner in which findings are introduced into policy debate.

Some experts have looked at the future of homicide rates and conclude that life in many cities will get riskier unless effective management of crime is realized.

Ideas about what is criminal are subject to shifts and changes and can be anticipated. But the kind of violent personal and property crime that we are primarily concerned about as antidevelopmental violates views of right and wrong that are held by almost all Americans, including most of the criminals themselves. This ethical base is not likely to change very much at all.

There are also likely to be future technical electronic and biological advances in crime management that will give many pause. Development and civil liberties organizations can be effective in maintaining a vigil over the future introduction and operation of these new devices and processes.

Some other analysts seem mildly optimistic about the future of American crime. They cite data collection improvements and population shifts as reasons for expecting some natural relief even without any particular effective policy response.

In development, a workable level of mass conformity with norms that support production, saving, and investment is important. It may be that the general American system can now afford to relax its discipline a bit after having entered the postindustrial age, although even this is questionable. However, Afro America, trying to achieve economic takeoff and accomplish its own belated "industrial revolution" can continue to encourage conformity to conventional productive norms of behavior to the year 2020.

Quality information on what the future may hold can be of great importance in influencing popular behavior. To the extent that some crime really is related to despair and frustration, people's expectations about the future and their chances to realize some satisfactions may be unrealistically low.

There is some basis for optimism. With sound organization and planning, hard work, political participation, intelligent leadership, and discipline much can be accomplished by many who now see only very limited prospects. But this positive vision has not been communicated widely or well by the leadership, and this failure may have much to do with current levels of crime and low levels of personal responsibility in segments of the population.

This is a somewhat circular phenomenon. Optimism and responsibility are required if there is to be an effective esprit de corps and sustained development. But development must be expected and believed in if personal responsibility and spirit are to be maintained. It is the role of the leadership to communicate accurately the full developmental potential regularly to all the people.

10 Internal Funding for Development

There are indications of growing interest in organized capital accumulation in Afro America. Groups hold frequent conferences to consider plans and programs that cannot be implemented for lack of funding. Those interested in the arts, political action, health, education, criminal justice, commercial development, and so on generate a constant stream of proposals. Many are worthwhile, and most call for ongoing financial support.

These activities underscore the need for increased savings in many forms and for organized fund raising and capital accumulation in well-planned, well-managed institutions.

Development requires harnessing financial resources. Saving and investment occur in many forms—commercial and noncommercial. Savings account deposits in financial institutions as well as the retained earnings of corporations contribute to savings. Indeed, increased savings in mattresses, socks, cookie jars, and piggy banks are also desirable if these ultimately find their way into institutions for investment and do not simply become deferred consumption. But interest here is in potential savings in the form of internal charity, or what might be thought of as voluntary taxation. Such savings will be an important component of any successful comprehensive development effort.

Events in the past decade have brought many people to realize that to accelerate development in their communities and institutions they must develop central treasuries.

There are several apparently effective national fund-raising efforts on behalf of Meharry Medical School, the United Negro College Fund (UNCF), the Voter Education Project, the NAACP Special Contributions Fund, and the NAACP Legal Defense and Education Fund among others. And from time to time there are one-shot appeals in legal emergencies or in support of the victims of natural disasters. But a requirement for an annual national program that successfully reaches and effectively appeals to all 7 to 8 million households and all the businesses still remains. A basic principle is clear: Afro America cannot permit itself to remain so financially dependent on government and established foundations and contributors for support of its ongoing or experimental programs. The NAA's financial crunch of 1976 illustrates the point.

Another example of financial vulnerability can be found in the experience of the community action efforts of the 1960s. In many places community organization was undertaken to develop cohesion and broader democratic participation. Energy was generated through rallies against traditional downtown political figures and institutions. Movement to oppose City Hall was generated over specific educational, service, or developmental issues. Some distortions, and even some demagoguery crept into these processes.

But City Hall perceived the threat, which, ironically, was funded by government. At the urging of many mayors, Congress withdrew financial support from community organizing.

That was predictable. It is now understood to be unrealistic to expect general institutions to underwrite consistently activities that conflict with the interests of the general system. If political organization is considered to have ongoing value, funds will have to be found internally.

Tithing requirements, such as in the Nation of Islam, have been the subject of comment. It has been reported that the expected level of support from adult members is 10 percent of income. Also, efforts like the "10–36" program of the Zion Baptist Church and the Reverend Leon Sullivan in Philadelphia have attracted attention. The church has organized a shopping center, various other commercial ventures, and some training programs using outside grants and leveraged equity capital raised largely from the 4,000-member congregation.

Historically, religious sanctions or charismatic leadership have succeeded in inducing savings increases by groups of people, who, because of relatively low incomes and other socioeconomic characteristics, would have been expected to consume virtually all income. Lower-income black people, like lower-income people in general, theoretically have high propensities to consume. But an effective appeal apparently can alter those patterns. The same may be true for middle-income households that, because of relentless advertising and other stimuli, also tend to have trouble saving consistently from year to year.

The national savings rate appears to be in the range of 7 to 10 percent annually. The Afro American rate appears to be lower than that in most years, although this is a complex subject. Some insight may be gained from Table 10-1. Notice that the comparison is between average family incomes. Since the upper range, the Top 20 percent of the income distribution, is very disproportionately white, the white average saving rate is pulled up.

According to Marcus Alexis, the highly regarded Northwestern economist, direct comparisons of savings by income categories suggest "evidence of higher savings (or lower dissavings) by blacks than by comparable income white families." And "statistical data show regional differences in savings. Northern blacks save a larger proportion of their incomes than Northern whites with the same incomes."[1]

Several hypotheses are available that attempt to explain these patterns. For development purposes, however, despite possibly greater household savings by black families of comparable incomes, the overall savings rate will have to increase as a proportion of total income if satisfactory development is to occur. The rate of 3 to 5 percent is probably too low for successful development. Of course the problem is compounded in that much of Afro America's saving does not occur in its financial institutions and is diverted away from its investments into investments in the general economy. Little of the reverse flow has occurred, although it may be possible to stimulate general savings in banks in Afro America as they gain in strength and numbers.

But the focus here is on a specific type of saving that occurs in the form of charitable donations. Some interracial flows of this kind do occur and presumably will continue. Black people give to general

Table 10-1
Comparative Savings, 1960–1961

	Black	White
Average after tax income	$3840	$6169
Current consumption	3707	5609
Savings	133	560
Savings as percentage of income	3.5	9.1

Source: adapted from Gardner Ackley, *Macroeconomic Theory* (New York: MacMillan & Co.), 1961, p. 247. Note also that the U.S. Census has not produced more recent comparative savings information since 1961, although the data have been collected.

system efforts such as the United Fund and Red Cross, and white people give to the UNCF and the NAA. There has been controversy over allocation decisions in United Fund budgets in several cities, and some reforms have been made. But even if the United Fund did everything that could reasonably be asked, there would still be a need for a similar autonomous organization managing a reservoir of funds for developmental program support—the National Fund.

Officials of United Way of America have not been enthusiastic at the prospect of a National Fund. Their cooperation and communication could be helpful to avoid undue abrasion.

There are issues on which it may be possible and desirable to develop something like "national" policies in Afro America. If so, such issues deserve serious research in independent centers or elsewhere, and that is costly. Similarly, problems in education, housing, health, employment, transportation, law enforcement, public safety, and economic development could be better addressed if institutions like Howard, Atlanta, and Fisk Universities, for example, could undertake more extensive research. Additional financial support to them, not just from alumni but from the broader community, perhaps through a National Fund, could help make that possible.

For these reasons and others, Afro America must increasingly fund its own development. Problems come quickly to mind concerning intragroup politics, personalities, collections, administration, disbursal, and safeguarding of large funds. There are difficulties to anticipate. But the basic problems are subject to demonstration and evaluative research.

The National Fund would contain elements similar to those of other national charitable organizations. The key problems will be recognized as marketing problems, which may be summarized as asking how to find a set of secular and technically effective substitutes for traditional charitable and religious commitment:

1. *Endorsement:* Who must vouch for the concept as well as the organization, national and local, that collects and distributes? How shall endorsement and visible participation be obtained from a sufficient range of development leaders, some of whom may, for practical reasons, feel initial uncertainty about associating with the National Fund?

Several major development organizations have budgets based on membership dues, general and corporate contributions, United Fund support, and government and foundation grants. The NAA and NUL are two of the strongest. They might be reluctant to take any short-run risks by associating with a fledgling National Fund. Some of their longstanding sources of budget support, such as the United Fund, might, for varying reasons, express displeasure at the emergence of the NF, viewing it as in some way competitive. But they can come to recognize that development requires a National Fund and cannot really succeed without it.

2. *Advertising:* In collaboration with the best professional fund raisers and advertising consultants, which media, what mix?

3. *Direct mail:* How intensive the solicitation?

4. *Broad base:* How extensive? How many households to reach directly in person and by mail—2, 4, 6, 8 million? How best to organize local campaigns and coordinate nationally? How best to use payroll checkoff through major employers?

5. *Appeal:* What will produce response? A request to *give,* or to *save,* or in some sense both? Or perhaps it can be presented as an opportunity to *invest* in progress and development. Or is it, after all, a matter of encouraging people to voluntarily *tax* themselves? Or would it be preferable to present it as an offer to consume, to *purchase* an intangible product—freedom, progress, security, development, and the like? Obviously there is considerable professional market research needed to develop a sustained massive National Fund.

As noted earlier the UNCF campaign slogan, "A Mind is a Terrible Thing to Waste," may be an effective appeal, for example. On the other hand, there may be more effective bases drawing on other perspectives about the role of higher education in development. The colleges are economic units. They produce human capital and in some cases applied research of great value. If they are primarily seen as places where individuals go to get the tools necessary for upward mobility then they may be given less public support than if they are projected as important cogs in a complex total economic development system. And their appeal might be vastly more successful if it found a way to focus attention on their institutional roles in furthering collective development rather than simply their function as training grounds for deserving low-income youngsters of large potential, important though that clearly is.

Many leaders express desire to see communitywide support for annual fund-raising drives to raise money from the community for the community. There is no obvious reason why this cannot be accomplished in this decade, although there are sources of opposition, apparently including some major foundations and executives of major national multipurpose funds. Their opposition is significant because they are in a position to make launching the National Fund either more or less difficult. Major foundations are especially important because operating budgets in the Fund's early phases will require significant grant subsidies.

A program officer at a very large foundation mentioned in private conversation that he had discussed the concept of providing a grant to subsidize the early operations of such a Fund. He reported that a senior executive of the foundation had reservations apparently based in part on his view that other groups had established fundraising programs without foundation support. Aside from questions of fact, the underlying skeptical attitude suggested here is important and will have to be successfully met.

What is the financial potential of the National Fund? It is difficult to judge, but it is worth looking at various combinations of assumptions on response and level of contribution. With conservative assumptions estimates can be derived in the $10 to $15 million range; with moderate assumptions, in the $20 to $30 million range; and, with optimistic ones, even higher, as can be seen in Table 10–2. Roughly, if we reckon total income in Afro America at over $60 billion, one-tenth of one percent of that is $60 million, and, given the savings rate, this might not be an unreasonable expectation after the Fund has achieved some operating history and wide respect as a sensible apparatus for internal development purposes.

A number of organizations have considered such a program. Indeed, there exists an effort known as the National Black United Fund that has sought to create a program together with several local funds now affiliated through it. It is headquartered in Los Angeles, and this may be a detriment relative to a Washington or New York alternative. And, as earlier noted, its name could be a subtle handicap. But it might nevertheless evolve into the vehicle for the National Fund.

The National Black United Fund may or may not be the proper vehicle around which to build a truly powerful National Fund. There are conceptual and organizational issues in the way the NBUF apparently has gone about its work in the early years that can make it difficult for the organization to become the instrument for launching The National Fund. The NBUF seems to give great emphasis to a

Table 10–2
Estimates of Total Potential of Coordinated Local Efforts in the National Fund

Number of Households in Millions[a]	Percentage Response	Total Contribution in Millions Estimated on the Basis of Average Contribution[b]						
		$10	$20	$30	$50	$75	$100	$200
2	10	2	4	6	10	15	20	40
	25	5	10	15	25	37.5	50	100
	50	10	20	30	50	75	100	200
4	10	4	8	12	20	30	40	80
	25	10	20	30	50	75	100	200
	50	20	40	60	100	150	200	400
6	10	6	12	18	30	45	60	120
	25	15	30	45	75	112.5	150	300
	50	30	60	90	150	225	300	600
8	10	8	16	24	40	60	80	160
	25	20	40	60	100	150	200	400
	50	40	80	120	200	300	400	800

[a]Effectively reached by mail, personal contact, or other initiative.

[b]Ten to twenty-five percent of these contributions would go to administration and fund-raising costs, depending on efficiency and management performance.

grass roots or community organizing thrust. Such a philosophy can be exaggerated to the detriment of successful broad-based fund raising and it can turn off those segments of the population with the greatest discretionary income and with the greatest concern about prudent management and scrupulous accountability. It is a reasonable assumption that middle-income households will respond to a first-rate, professional campaign with contributions in the $100 to $200 range each year. And these same people may give only a few dollars, to avoid a hassle, with a campaign that has the appearance of a grass roots or people's campaign. That may simply turn out to be a market reality that will have to be respected.

Volunteer participation and local initiative would be important elements in The National Fund, but they probably would not become matters of primary philosophical commitment. Fund raising is the objective, not community action, and a businesslike, marketing-oriented approach is most likely to be superior in reaching those households and institutions with the most accessible discretionary income. The purpose is to raise very large sums of money to support prudent and efficiently managed programs and projects. It is a matter of management, not sociology or social work, and too much of the latter orientation could tend to inhibit the development of a strong National Fund.

It takes money to raise money. Proper funding is required from the start. A guesstimate is that adequate capitalization for a three-year national test of this approach to internal fund raising would be on the order of $5 to $10 million. That is, staff, marketing and fund raising consulting fees, computer charges, overhead and administration, and the costs of direct mail and media would be in that range to do a proper job of getting the project underway. A combination of private one-shot contributions, corporate and foundation grants, government grants, especially from EDA, and loans would be the initial capital structure. Some of the loans could be arranged on a commercial self-liquidating basis. This element allows leverage on the grants and also would supply some extra financial discipline.

The NAA and the NUL have budgets provided for by membership dues, general and corporate contributions, United Fund support and government and foundation grants. They might be reluctant to take any short-run risks by associating with a fledgling National Fund out of concern that some of their long-standing sources of budget support, such as the United Way, might, for various reasons, express displeasure at the emergence of The National Fund, viewing it as in some way competitive. So there could be some diplomatic problems in bringing the NAA and the NUL into the project at an early stage. But their participation can be of great significance so early discussions with them are important.

In any event, problems of coordination and cooperation in the National Fund may strike some as staggering. It is no secret that there have been, historically, problems of mutual trust, respect, and cooperation. It is reasonable to assume for now that they are manageable, if not solvable.

The lesson is clear: It takes money to raise money.[2] The catalytic agent to raise seed money to establish the structure and launch the Fund perhaps could be a business-oriented group, a group of development leaders, athletes, and entertainers[3] —frequently mentioned as people looking for ways to make a worthwhile contribution to development, or religious leaders. Such a group may exist, but more likely it needs to be created.

A coalition of three or four major development organizations is perhaps the ideal sponsorship. A major benefit will be its pressure toward program development. The Fund presumably will screen applications for financial assistance according to serious standards of feasibility and soundness.

The National Fund can lead to greater emphasis on careful program development by groups all along the ideological spectrum. Its success can accelerate planning and growth throughout the developing system.

Notes

1. Marcus Alexis, "Patterns of Black Consumption," *Journal of Black Studies,* September 1970, pp. 59–63. See also Marcus Alexis, "Wealth Accumulation of Black Families: The Empirical Evidence: Comment," paper presented at a joint session of the American Economic Association and the American Finance Association, 1970.

2. Government agencies such as Economic Development Administration, Treasury Department, HEW, or others could be a source for a large, multimillion dollar demonstration grant to commence operations in the Fund. The National Fund once in successful operation for a few years would represent an extraordinarily efficient and high-leverage use of federal grant capital to promote self help and self sufficiency. Determining the right agency and the right approach to a timely grant application for a novel program is a responsibility for the development leadership. It might be preferable to avoid the bureaucracy altogether, but federal monies for this start-up effort do seem justified.

3. Many show business and sports figures have become associated with images of extravagant living and conspicuous consumption. This is unfortunate. Afro America probably needs a decade or so of voluntary semiausterity to develop rapidly.

Several noted high-income athletes and entertainers have made a public point of their intention to initiate or carry out personal charitable programs. Muhammed Ali, Arthur Ashe, Kareem Abdul Jabbar, James Brown, Bill Cosby, Melvin Van Peebles, and Jim Brown are some of those who come to mind. Other candidates for a founders group might include Hank Aaron, James Baldwin, Harry Belafonte, Diahann Carroll, Wilt Chamberlain, Miles Davis, Ossie Davis, Sammy Davis, Jr., Ruby Dee, Julius Erving, Redd Foxx, Joe Frazier, A.G. Gaston, Marvin Gaye; also, Calvin Hill, Jesse Hill, the Jackson Family, Reggie Jackson, George Johnson, John Johnson, James Earl Jones, Quincy Jones, Gladys Knight, Johnny Mathis, Curtis Mayfield, Willie Mays, George McGinnis, Joe Morgan, Sidney Poitier, Leontyne Price, Charlie Pride, Richard Pryor, Diana Ross, Richard Roundtree, Bill Russell, O.J. Simpson, Asa Spaulding, Sarah Vaughan, Cicely Tyson, Billy Dee Williams, Fred Williamson, Flip Wilson and Frank Yerby.

Fifty such persons at $20,000 each could be an effective foundation group for a National Fund. A carefully planned, one-shot contribution of $1 million from them could be matched with grants from foundations and others and could provide an effective initial operating capitalization for the Fund.

This group could thereby help make possible the mechanism through which the 25 million people in Afro America can thereafter systematically look after more of their own development requirements.

11

Managing the Research and Consulting Process

Substantial publicly funded and privately managed technoeconomic social science research bears on economic development. Much contract research and related consulting goes unnoticed by any private development organizations or by any elected officials apart from those directly concerned. The public interest and community and developmental interests may be better served by greater attention by leaders of development to these research and consulting processes.

Progress in Afro America has depended significantly on organization and application of information and knowledge. This will be true even more over the next several decades.

Research and consulting will be important in private and public policy and program development. In the last ten years local development leaders have become more sophisticated about how government affects their development efforts. But there is a lag in recognition of dangers posed by at least some practices and attitudes in some, and perhaps many, research and consulting organizations. Administered and legislated reforms may be in order to insure that research and consulting processes better serve the public interest and that development efforts are not stymied by distortions in research processes.

The knowledge industry includes many organizations in addition to its principal institutions, colleges, and universities. Attention here is on research and consulting firms, profit and nonprofit. These are engaged in applied research in the social sciences. University research on sensitive, value-laden issues has, however, stirred controversy and some appears, to many observers, to have even had hostile social motivations.

Development organizations, the NAA and NUL, together with agencies like NAACP Legal Defense and Educational Fund, and professional associations of psychologists, sociologists, economists, engineers, educators, lawyers, and scientists can monitor research activities that bear on development interests. They have the Freedom of Information Act to provide access to publicly funded nonclassified research. They also have such diverse instruments as the Equal Employment Opportunity Act, the Consumer Affairs Section of the Antitrust Division of the Department of Justice, state and local freedom of information statutes, and legal action including litigation to gain access to research believed harmful in content, faulty in execution, or threatening in implication or potential government application.

The Knowledge Industry

Nonprofit organizations active in urban and social research include well known institutions such as RAND Corporation, Stanford Research Institute, and Battelle Memorial Institute. Specialized organizations like the Brookings Institution, the Hudson Institute, and the Institute for the Future are also factors and deserve scrutiny. There are also profit-oriented firms such as Arthur D. Little, of Cambridge, Massachusetts, Planning Research Corporation in Los Angeles, and others.

General consulting firms like Booz, Allen and Hamilton and McKinsey and Company, Inc., are active in development-related and public policy research. Large public accounting firms like Arthur Anderson, Price Waterhouse, Peat Marwick and Mitchell, and Coopers and Lybrand are also engaged in applied social science research and consulting for private and public clients.

Planning consultants and economic consultants also do important work. Engineering consultants are active, as are architect and landscape architect firms from time to time. Public opinion and survey research firms also are engaged in work that often goes with little public notice. Lastly, heavy industrial companies, for example in metals, aerospace, and forest products such as Alcoa, General Electric, Lockheed, and Boise Cascade have been similarly active.

The principal interest here is in the first two groups, and some extra attention is due those firms that emphasize applying to social policy and development issues analytical systems first used in the context of strategic or defense analysis.

Although each organization is unique, a closer look at one may provide insights of general value. Stanford Research Institute is a 29-year-old not-for-profit research organization with headquarters outside San Francisco in Menlo Park, California. It was founded after

World War II by West Coast industrialists who foresaw the need for independent applied research in the sciences and in technoeconomics to support economic development in the eleven western states.

SRI has a staff of about 1500 professionals. It works in almost every science and social science discipline. It has offices and project teams around the world and across the United States. In recent years it does over $70 million in contract research annually.

Quality of work in an organization like this varies according to the individuals working on each project, and it is sometimes influenced by factors outside the control of researchers, such as contract renegotiations affecting available resources and unanticipated changes in time to complete. In general, technical quality is good, and there are staff members with national and international reputations, as is true of other large research and consulting organizations.

SRI has an Urban and Social Systems Department as well as other groups working in housing, education, transportation, economic development, and other issues of developmental significance. Such work bears greater attention from development organizations. If there is reason to believe there could be significant social bias in any of these value-laden investigations, then a systematic review process by development oversight organizations could be appropriate to protect the process of policy formation on development issues from contamination through social bias.

Research organizations like SRI have in important professional and managerial positions some senior people whose personal attitudes on social and development issues bear scrutiny. It is not unfair to say that some are concerned with maintaining relative social distributions of income, wealth, status, and policy influence roughly as they have known them through most of their lives. To the extent this is true, their influence on policy research and formulation can be of interest to watchful professional, public interest, and development organizations.

These professionals are technically well qualified, in most cases, and their racial, social, and political views are not expressed in uniformly or consistently biased ways. Most would profess, for example, concern about a wide range of matters of social dysfunction. Few would condone common social discrimination in employment or fiscal allocation matters. Indeed, many would appear to be liberals in the usual popular sense. But consultants and policy analysts who have personal social biases in favor of government's minimal or nonintervention in behalf of parity for the developing systems deserve close attention. Though they may present consistent technically serious justifications they are often unable to completely disguise fundamental social bias. Experts and analysts—dispassionate and objective investigators, when subject to penetrating and close questioning and review—will often reveal social bias or even in some cases hostility, despite efforts at concealment. If such attitudes exist in persons able to influence policy, then it serves the public interest to have them disclosed.

Development and oversight organizations such as the National Urban League and the NAA can take note of large public contracts and seek to have knowledgeable representatives speak to contracting officers, review proposals, and interview principal investigators. Such procedures, made regular, could have substantial beneficial effects on policy research processes. Professional organizations like the National Medical Association, National Bar Association, and National Economics Association could also establish research review committees to pay attention to contract research processes.

Research and consulting firms like SRI generally maintain fairly high degrees of staff professional integrity. But integrity, that is, basic technical honesty, is not incompatible with social bias in the conduct of research. There can even be technically honest bigotry.

There is also a certain technical narrowness, more common at senior than at junior levels, expressed in a tendency to ignore or minimize the importance of what are considered "noneconomic" factors in project or policy analysis. The practical effect of this posture has often been to exclude from analysis negative social consequences for the developing systems. A narrow definition of costs and benefits results frequently in failure to consider adverse impacts of public works projects, for example, on developing systems. Comprehensive attention to social, political, psychological, cultural, and aesthetic considerations has been increasing in the last several years, and such oversights are now diminished. Nevertheless, some process of research review by development organizations and their designated specialist representatives can help. Studies for such agencies as HUD, DOT, FRB, HEW, DOD, DOL, SBA, and so forth, are often begun and completed with little or no public awareness or scrutiny.

The proposition to this point is that a responsible private external developmental review process is desirable because of a tendency to personal social bias among some senior professionals and managers in contract research and consulting organizations. In addition to social bias there are philosophical positions, honestly held, but of dubious or arguable merit, that may be of legitimate concern to leaders of development as well.

Some senior professionals and managers are "good government" advocates whose principal criterion of good government is efficiency in a narrow sense, with little reference to such other values as equity, responsiveness, or openness. This view can lead, for example, to a commitment to metropolitan or regional government because of expected realization of scale economies. This commitment becomes, in some instances, an article of faith. Regional government has political consequences that tend to favor some groups more than others. Researchers who pretend neutrality on the political outcomes of regionalization may be fairly viewed with skepticism. So may those who claim disinterest in political and social consequences of analytically based policy recommendations.

In addition to an attraction for regionalization, some senior policy analysts are intrigued with ideas of dispersal of low-scale social groups as a solution to certain persistent policy problems. This preference, in some, has the character of a social reflex reaction against demographic patterns that they find personally undesirable rather than the result of a responsible analysis of a range of policy choices. If this is the case, it ought to be made explicit, so that clients can know what is advocacy and what is not.

A further possible source of bias in social policy analysis is the phenomenon of transfer of skills of surplus aerospace and defense analysts to social policy projects. Some large contract organizations have sought to employ excess analytical capacity on newly acquired nondefense contracts in housing, criminal justice, education, health, transportation, business development, and the like. Some of these analysts are capable of making a smooth transition and a worthwhile contribution. Others, however, are bringing many years of hard-line ideological preoccupations along with their technical skills, and become in effect, contaminating agents in social policy and developmental matters. Their political and social policy preferences are often decidedly hostile to lower-scale groups and to the aspirations of the developing systems. Their participation in policy and program analysis introduces a social supremacist point of view that ought not escape detection by development organizations.

Development organizations can invite senior staff of research and consulting firms to participate in panel discussions. In these forums those who are hostile can be identified. Under careful questioning, harmful or dysfunctional social attitudes will emerge, and steps can then be taken to, in effect, quarantine these firms until they adjust their staffs.

Bias can also be introduced into policy research because of commercial realities. Desires to receive "follow on" or next and related contracts can produce willingness to compromise research by modifying conclusions or recommendations to keep clients happy or at least unembarrassed.

Most professionals consider themselves objective and unbiased. Most would deny that any analyst should be an explicit advocate for any group's interests. But it is widely perceived by professionals and lay people alike, that all Americans who work on social policy analysis are advocates in some manner. Every American has an interest and a stake of some kind in the outcome of that set of contests commonly summarized as the social issue, and each advocates, more or less actively, the status quo, small change, or major change in some direction. Many senior professionals in research and consulting seem to favor either the first or second alternative. Those leaders and organizations who favor more substantial changes, and seek to promote sustained development therefore have some interest in paying attention to the policy work of analytical professionals.

There are other aspects of structure or scope of work in some research and consulting firms that may also introduce bias into value-laden development-related studies. First, some do work in South Africa, for the government in some cases, and for corporations in others. Second, some firms work in the United States on a variety of internal security matters for law enforcement and intelligence agencies, federal, state, and local. Legitimate work in both fields is possible, but, as it happens, some work in both fields has origins hostile to the aspirations and interests of the developing systems. The practical question is, can organizations that do work that is basically hostile in this way at the same time work for other clients and help development? This is an open issue. Public interest and development organizations can consider it as they review the practices of individual firms.

The social composition of boards of directors or trustees, and of professional staffs may also influence the direction and conduct of research and consulting programs. Some firms work on value-laden, development-related issues and carry out these assignments with socially homogeneous staffs. Biased results may be more likely under these circumstances, and external examination, and perhaps legal intervention may help to prevent bias from these sources influencing public policy.

This review of research and consulting points to possible abuses and sources of systematic social bias. Further investigation can be institutionalized in private development oversight organizations. Continuing vigilance can help protect Afro America from the hostility of some in the professional research community. And it can insure that all the other difficult work of development is not offset or diminished by opponents operating under the respectable cover of professional consulting and social science.

12 Conclusion

When most academic experts, business leaders, government officials, politicians, journalists, and other quoted citizens speak of the problems of the cities, or domestic social problems, they are, by and large, really speaking of the problem of how to develop Afro America. Many, if not most, would recoil from that suggestion, and would downplay racial dimensions in favor of emphasis on finding a set of sound policies that can be efficiently employed to better the lives and prospects of all people. That is fair enough as a guiding principle for public policy in a complex multiethnic society like the United States, but analytically, development in Afro America is the crux of the matter.

Leaders in Afro America and their colleagues and allies in the general American system can adopt a development point of view in approaching urban and social problems. And they can become more cognizant of income and wealth redistributive implications in proposals on housing, education, employment and human resources, general monetary and fiscal policy, and on small business development.

The idea of systematically transferring assets in the form of going concerns from the general to the developing systems, for example, is going to take a while to become palatable. But it is a sensible way to accelerate development, and it is justified on equity grounds—and very likely on efficiency grounds as well. Similarly, using antitrust philosophy to restructure some sectors of the American economy along fairer social lines will seem esoteric at first, but it will gradually commend itself as a legitimate use of regulatory mechanisms.

Crime makes just about everybody unhappy. And it is not likely that society will tolerate random abuse and predatory violence much longer. The development leadership can recognize that as a practical matter they are able to take creative steps to manage this problem, and to take initiatives in bringing large urban areas and small towns back to conditions of order and normal levels of safety.

The National Fund will help the leadership do many things now annually proposed but not done because of resource scarcity. Without the Fund, development objectives will be very seriously delayed in being realized, and there are few projects that can be established so quickly—say, in two to three years—that can have such great long-term payoffs. It is hard to think of any single project that could deserve a higher immediate priority with the leaders of major development organizations.

Alertness to processes of research and consulting will be repaid with fewer frustrated and undermined policy proposals. Opposition will not appear to be so mysterious or sudden. There have, of course, been efforts to establish and maintain think tanks and research centers, and some have been more or less successful. But one or two of first-rate quality would be of disproportionate significance in protecting development interests, in advancing development points of view, and in providing the leadership with better and more timely analyses so they might avoid conceptual dead ends on difficult contested policy questions. On such complex issues as busing, and affirmative action, for example, they might be better off had they had the benefit, early on, of consistent, thorough, farsighted, and comprehensive policy analysis and research, undertaken under auspices in Afro America and not dependent on sanction and support from institutions in the general system.

The constant and inevitable clash of interests on social policy and resource allocation questions is effectively expressed, by some, through crucial influence or even control of important communications instruments. Those who consistently seem to prevail in policy disputes on race-related questions are apparently well connected in the editorial offices of major newspapers, publishers, television stations and networks, and at a handful of highly respected magazines and journals. The leadership is going to have to find ways to consistently get its point of view into the formation of policy opinion early and effectively. Writing and speaking in the existing channels of the general system is one way. However, on the crucial redistributive and developmental issues, the principal opinion makers, editors, and commentators, of the general system are often arrayed against those of the Afro-American system. For the latter to have a real chance of making persuasive and timely presentations, therefore, they will have to be able to count on responsive editorial ears. Where is the most likely place for such receptivity to be found? Clearly, the answer is in small, high-quality journals and magazines established with their assistance, or at their initiative. One first-rate weekly, monthly, bi-monthly, and quarterly, together with one solid daily, if that difficult task can be accomplished, can make the process of development smoother and more rational. Without the creation of at least some of these organs, the leadership is going to continue to find itself consistently beaten to the draw on controversial issues by the academic and policy intellectual elite of the general American system. Afro-American writers with something insightful and constructive to say should not always have to turn to the editorial offices of the *New York Times Magazine, The Public Interest, Harpers, Harvard Business Review,* and *The Atlantic,* for example, to receive a timely and respectful airing of ideas. Those editors, solid professionals though they are, have interests to protect, and points of view to advance, and the development point of view is often in conflict with theirs. Development depends on an effective and savvy participation in the policy influence process. It is hard to think of any other project that so deserves to be ranked almost on a par with the creation of the National Fund as does the creation of serious monthly or quarterly journals of policy review and initiative. Development, again, will be seriously handicapped without them.

The press in Afro America, especially the big city weeklies and twice-weeklies, deserve continuing impartial impersonal scrutiny and criticism. Their practices, often sensational and cynical, can be a detriment to development. As a practical matter they have to sell papers, but there is reason to believe there are other and better ways.

And now a cautious word about the role of religious leaders and the major protestant denominations. The church and its leaders have, by general agreement, seen the people of Afro America through some difficult and treacherous times. And it continues, in many instances, to be a rock, a sure foundation for constructing the developing system. However, a good deal of religious activity, and church leadership specifically, appears to be thoughtless, and has about it an undisciplined, and even, perhaps, an intellectually irresponsible quality that leads to emphasis on transitory feeling and avoidance of care and planning in day-to-day life. Many ministers, by virtue of this misplaced emphasis, are doing the community a disservice and are unsuited by training or temperament to lead or encourage their members to self development or community growth and prosperity. This is not a blanket charge. And it is not based on survey research or close analysis. It is a strong impression and is not uncommon. The issue deserves a thorough and sustained examination. But if broad-based and comprehensive development is desired by the great majority of the people, then attention will have to be paid to those habits and practices and institutions that have a counterdevelopmental thrust. Some aspects of some of the traditional religious life deserve scrutiny in this context. Responsible analysis of this issue would be enhanced through open discussion in just such magazines and journals as have been identified as absent. Without some reform in the training and behavior of many ministers—a significant minority of the clergy—development will take a longer time in being realized than it might otherwise.

Development, finally, needs personal champions and spokespersons—articulators of a vision—just as civil rights did. It is true that the development process is a highly complex and technical business with less room for heroics and emotion and rhetoric. And it is true that too much emphasis has in the past been put on the charismatic leader. Those lessons, presumably, have been learned. Careful planning, and sophisticated, disciplined managerial processes can now be employed to produce developmental gains just as in any other developing system.

Despite the technocratic nature of the undertaking, however, there is room for visionary leadership. Hopefully, out of the disparate elements in the development leadership, two or three will emerge who are technically competent and also somewhat charismatic, whose persuasive call and reasoned articulation will give an extra dimension to organized and planned activities. They will inspire an adequate effort and sufficient cooperation and mutual support to accomplish reasonable development objectives by the year 2020.

Selected Bibliography

Amara, Roy C. "Toward a Framework for National Goals and Policy Research." *Policy Sciences,* March 1972, p. 59–70.

Andenaes, Johannes. "The Moral or Educative Influence of Criminal Law." *The Journal of Social Issues,* vol. 27 no. 2, 1971, pp. 17–32.

Anderson, Charles A. "New Types of R&D Organizations: The Not for Profit Research Institutes." *Vital Speeches,* October 5, 1975, pp. 15–17.

Angrist, Shirley S. "Is Sociology A Policy Science?" *Sociological Focus,* October 1975, pp. 383–386.

Baritz, L. *The Servants of Power: A History of the Use of Social Science in American Industry.* Middletown, Conn.: Wesleyan University Press, 1960.

Beals, Ralph L. "Who Will Rule Research?" *Psychology Today,* September, 1970.

Bell, Daniel, "The Study of the Future; Can One Predict?" *The Public Interest,* no. 1, Fall 1965, p. 119.

Benveniste, Guy, *The Politics of Expertise.* San Francisco: The Glendessary Press, 1972.

Bernstein, Ilene N. and Freeman, Howard F. *Academic and Entreprenuerial Research; The Consequences of Diversity in Federal Evaluation Studies,* New York: Russell Sage Foundation, 1975.

Bernstein, Ilene, ed. "Validity Issues in Evaluative Research." *Sociological Methods & Research,* August 1975.

Bernstein, Samuel; Ferber, Roman; and Bernstein, A. Isaac. "The Problems and Pitfalls of Quantitative Methods in Urban Analysis." *Policy Sciences,* March 1973, pp. 29–40.

Bickman, Leonard. "Bystander Intervention in a Crime: The Effects of a Mass Media Campaign." *Journal of Applied Social Psychology,* Oct–Dec 1975, pp. 296–302.

Bogdan, Robert. "Conducting Evaluation Research—Integrity Intact." *Sociological Focus,* January 1976, pp. 63–72.

Boulding, Kenneth E. "The Future of Personal Responsibility," *American Behavioral Scientist,* January–February 1972, pp. 329–360.

Burns, Maywood. "Black People and the Tyranny of American Law." *The Annals,* January 1976.

99

Charlesworth, James C., ed. "Integration of the Social Sciences Through Policy Analysis." *The Annals of the American Academy of Political and Social Science,* October 1972.

(Clark), Cedric X, ed. "The White Researcher in Black Society." *The Journal of Social Issues,* vol. 29, no. 1, 1973.

Crockett, Stanley. "The Role of the Researcher in Educational Settings: Perspectives on Research and Evaluation." *Journal of Social Issues,* vol. 29, no. 1, 1973, pp. 81–85.

Danziger, Sheldon and Wheeler, David. "The Economics of Crime: Punishment or Income Redistribution." *Review of Social Economy,* October 1975.

Davis, John A. "Justification for No Obligation: Views of Black Males Toward Crime and the Criminal Law." *Issues in Criminology,* Fall 1974, pp. 69–87.

Dillingham, Gerald. "Black Attitudes Toward Police and the Courts." *Black World,* December 1974, pp. 4–13.

Dotson, A. Bruce. "Social Planning and Urban Violence." *Urban Affairs Quarterly,* March 1974, pp. 283–302.

Dror, Yehezkel. "Policy Sciences: Some Global Perspectives." *Policy Sciences,* March 1974, pp. 83–88.

Dunning, Roosevelt. "Black on Black Crime." *Vital Speeches,* January 15, 1976, pp. 215–217.

Duncan, Otis Dudley. "Social Forecasting—The State of the Art." *The Public Interest,* no. 17, Fall 1969, p. 88.

Elkin, Stephen L. "Political Science and the Analysis of Public Policy." *Public Policy,* Summer 1974, p. 399.

Etzioni, Amitai. "An Engineer-Social Science Team at Work." *The International Journal of Research Management,* January 1976, pp. 18–22.

Friesema, H. Paul. "Urban Studies and Action Research." *Urban Affairs Quarterly,* September 1971, p. 3–12.

Gahringer, R.E. "Punishment and Responsibility." *The Journal of Philosophy,* May 1969, pp. 291–306.

Gastil, Raymond D. "Social Humanities." *Policy Science,* March 1974, pp. 1–14.

Gaston, Jerry and Sherohman, James. "Origins of Researchers on Black Americans." *The American Sociologist,* May 1974, pp. 75–82.

Goland, Martin. "Public Attitudes Toward Technology—Enlightened or Disruptive." *Journal of the Society of Research Administrators,* January 1976, pp. 12–18.

Goodwin, Leonard. "The Relation of Social Research to Practical Affairs." *The Journal of Applied Behavioral Science,* January–March 1975, p. 7–13.

Greenberg, Daniel S. "The Myth of the Scientific Elite." *The Public Interest,* no. 1, Fall 1965, p. 51.

Hambriek, Ralph. "A Guide for the Analysis of Policy Arguments." *Policy Sciences,* December 1974, pp. 469–578.

Harman, Willis W. "On Normative Futures Research." *Policy Sciences,* June 1975, pp. 121–136.

_____. "The Great Legitimacy Challenge." *Vital Speeches,* December 15, 1975, pp. 147–149.

Higginbotham, A. Leon. "Racism and the Early American Legal Process, 1619–1896." *The Annals,* January 1976.

Hindelang, Michael. "Moral Evaluations of Illegal Behaviors." *Social Problems.* vol. 21, no. 3, pp. 370–884.

Hohorst, Henry G. "The Corporate Contribution." *Saturday Review,* January 13, 1968, p. 56.

Holland, R. William. "White Researchers in Black America: The Epistemological Boondoggle." *Public Policy.*

Hopkins, Andrew. "On the Sociology of Criminal Law." *Social Problems,* June 1975, pp. 608–619.

Horowitz, Irving Louis, ed. "The Rise and Fall of Project Camelot Studies," *The Relationship Between Social Science and Practical Politics.* Cambridge, Mass.: MIT Press, 1967.

Kaplan, Abraham. "On the Strategy of Social Planning." *Policy Sciences,* March 1973, p. 41–62.

King, Martin Luther, Jr. "The Role of the Behavioral Scientist in the Civil Rights Movement." *American Psychologist,* vol. 23, no. 2, 1968, p. 180.

Koch, E.L. "School Vandalism and Strategies of Social Control." *Urban Education,* April 1975, pp. 54–72.

Levin, Martin A. and Dornbusch, Horst D. "Pure and Policy Social Science: Evaluation of Policies in Criminal Justice and Education." *Public Policy,* Winter 1973, pp. 383–424.

Levine, James P. "The Ineffectiveness of Adding Police to Prevent Crime." *Public Policy,* Fall 1975, pp. 523–545.

Long, Norton E. "Let's Not Confuse Public Sector Research With

Public Relations." *Public Administration Review,* July/August 1972, pp. 347, 348.

McCleary, Roland D. "Violent Youth." *International Journal of Offender Therapy and Comparative Criminology,* vol. 19, no. 1, 1975, pp. 81–86.

Meier, Anne. "The Governmental Research and Development Market." SRI paper presented at the 43rd National Conference of the American Marketing Association, Minneapolis, Minnesota, June 15–17, 1970.

Meltsner, Arnold J. "Political Feasibility and Policy Analysis." *Public Administration Review,* November/December 1972, pp. 859–867.

Morehouse, Thomas A. "Program Evaluation: Social Research v. Public Policy." *Public Administration Review,* November/December 1972, pp. 868–874.

Nelson, Carl W. "Management Consultants in Non-Profit Organizations, A Survey, Discussion, and Recommendations." *Business Perspectives,* Summer 1973, pp. 12–15.

Nelson, Richard. "Intellectualizing about the Moon–Ghetto Metaphor; A Study of the Current Malaise of Rational Analysis of Social Problems." *Policy Sciences,* December 1974, pp. 375–414.

Orlans, Harold. "The Political Uses of Social Research." *The Annals of the American Academy of Political and Social Science,* March 1971, pp. 28–35.

_____. "Neutrality and Advocacy in Policy Research." *Policy Sciences,* June 1975, pp. 107–120.

Orleans, Peter and Ellis, William Russell, Jr., eds. *Race, Change and Urban Society.* Beverly Hills: Sage Publications, 1971. See especially Edward L. Paynter, "Power in the Reformulation of Race Research."

Reid, Inez Smith. "Science, Politics, and Race." *Signs; Journal of Women in Culture and Society,* Winter 1975, pp. 397–422.

Rein, Martin. "Social Policy Analysis as the Interpretation of Beliefs." *Journal of the American Institute of Planners,* September 1971, pp. 297–310.

Relyea, Harold O. "Opening Government to Public Scrutiny: A Decade of Federal Efforts." *Public Administration Review,* January/February 1975, pp. 3–10.

Redburn, Thomas, "Open Files: Letting Exxon In." *The Washington Monthly,* July–August, 1975, pp. 18–21.

Saloschin, Robert L. "The Freedom of Information Act: A Government Perspective." *Public Administration Review,* January/February 1975, pp. 10–14.

Saunders, Lonnie. "Effective Control of Urban Crime: Mission Immpossible." *The Crisis,* March 1974.

Scott, Robert A. and Shore, Arnold. "Sociology and Policy Analysis." *American Sociologist,* May 1974.

Shils, Willie, Edelman; et al. "New Styles in Social Research." *Society,* July/August 1975.

Sjoberg, Gideon and Littrel, W. Boyd, eds. "Social Control of Social Research." *Social Problems,* Summer 1973.

Smith, Thomas B. "Policy Roles: An Analysis of Policy Formulators and Policy Implementors." *Policy Sciences,* September 1973, pp. 297–308.

Streeten, Paul P. "Social Science Research on Development: Some Problems in the Use and Transfer of an Intellectual Technology." *Journal of Economic Literature,* December 1974, pp. 1290–1300.

Tribe, Lawrence H. "Policy Science: Analysis of Ideology, Philosophy." *Public Affairs,* Fall 1972, pp. 66–110.

Vickers, Geoffrey. "Values, Norms and Policies." *Policy Sciences,* March 1973, pp. 103–112.

Wilkins, Leslie T. "Crime and Criminal Justice at the Turn of the Century." *The Annals,* January 1976.

Williams, Walter. "The Capacity of Social Science Organizations to Perform Large-Scale Evaluative Research." *Urban Affairs Quarterly,* June 1972, pp. 431–472.

Wolf, Eleanor P. "Social Science and Social Policy: Social Science and the Courts: The Detroit School Case." *The Public Interest,* Winter, 1976, pp. 102–120.

Index

About the Author

Richard F. America is an independent consultant, researcher, and writer in Washington, D.C. He received the B.S. in Business Administration majoring in economics from Pennsylvania State University, and the M.B.A. from Harvard Business School. After 4 years on the urban economics staff at Stanford Research Institute, he spent three years as Director of Urban Programs at the Schools of Business Administration, at the University of California at Berkeley where he was also a lecturer in Business Administration. He has also been a visiting lecturer at Stanford Business School. Mr. America has contributed to professional journals on policy issues in the economic development of Afro America, and has been a member of the staff of the House Banking Committee and a consultant to the Congressional Budget Office. He is coauthor with Professor Bernard Anderson of the Wharton School of *Conversations on Management: Black Managers in Large Organizations,* forthcoming.